RAINCOAST CHRONICLES

Sixteen

TIME & TIDE:
A HISTORY OF TELEGRAPH COVE

PAT WASTELL NORRIS

HARBOUR

In Memory of Telegraph Cove

I am grateful to my mother and my grandfather for leaving their memories behind, and to Jimmy and
Thelma Burton for sharing theirs with me

Pat Norris

Copyright © 1995 by Pat Wastell Norris
All rights reserved.

Published by:
Harbour Publishing Co. Ltd
P.O. Box 219
Madeira Park, BC, VON 2H0

Cover, page design and composition: Lionel Trudel, Aspect Design

Photograph of Pat Norris by Cristel Nottelman. All other photographs courtesy of the author, except
for page 64 courtesy of Jimmy Burton, p. 55 courtesy of Jimmy Burton and Liv Kennedy, p. 44
courtesy of Harbour Publishing, and p. 84 by Jim Borrowman courtesy of Liv Kennedy. Photo of SS
Cassiar on p. 12 by Walter E. Frost, City of Vancouver Archives. Map of Telegraph Cove area and
illustration on p. 18 by Lionel Trudel.
Excerpt from *Whistle Up the Inlet*, © 1984 by Gerald Rushton, reprinted by permission of Douglas
& MacIntyre.

Published with the assistance of the Canada Council, the Publications Assistance Program of BC
Heritage Trust, and the Cultural Services Branch of the Government of BC's Tourism and Ministry
Responsible for Culture.

Printed and bound in Canada.

Canadian Cataloguing in Publication Data

Norris, Pat Wastell
Raincoast chronicles #16

ISBN 1-55017-121-6

1. Telegraph Cove (B.C.)--History. 2. Sawmills--British Columbia--Vancouver
Island. I. Title. II. Title: Raincoast chronicles sixteen. III. Title: Time and tide.
FC 3849.T44N67 1995   971.1'2   C95-910171-3
F1089.5.T44N67 1995

RAINCOAST CHRONICLES

Sixteen

TABLE OF CONTENTS

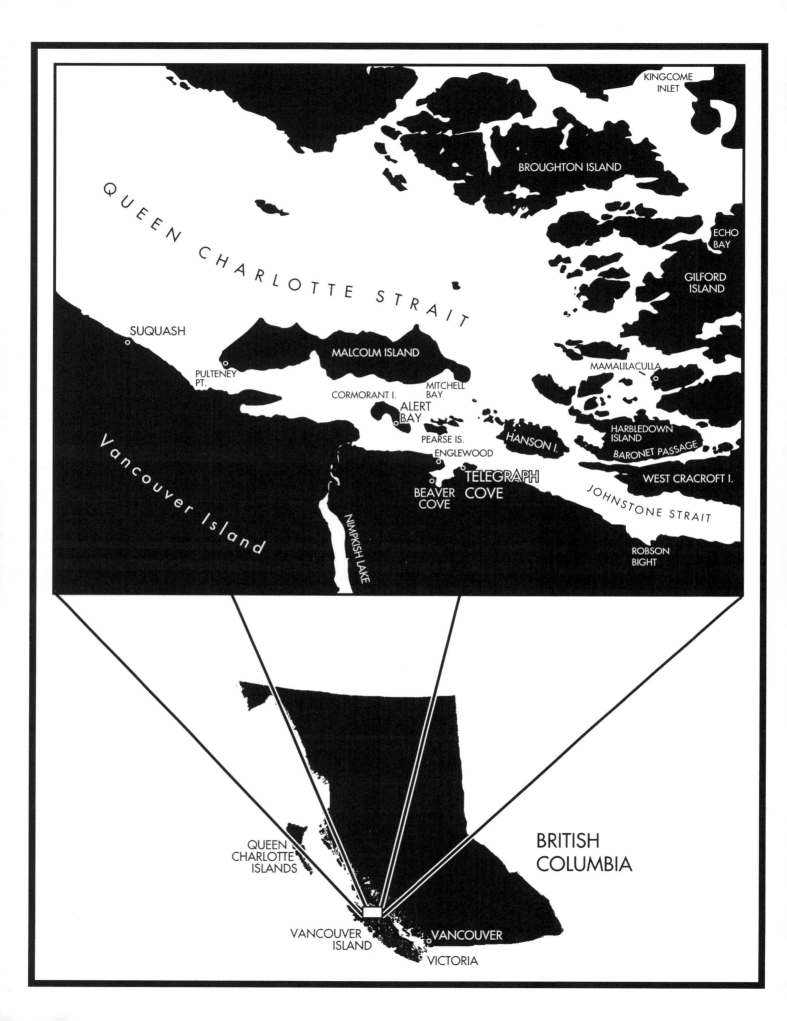

Telegraph Cove ranks as one of the notable man-made landmarks of the BC Coast, a tiny notch in the desolate Vancouver Island coastline between Kelsey Bay and Port McNeill almost totally encircled by an elaborate system of boardwalks and wooden buildings built on shorefront pilings. It is a *tour de force* of barnacled architecture, a kind of accidental gumboot theme park. A first-comer to Telegraph Cove feels just a tiny bit like a first-time visitor to Venice: the natural landscape has been taken over by a structure of great elaborateness, but there is scarcely a clue left as to who made it and to what purpose. The mystery is made more enticing by the feeling something remarkable must have gone on here, to have left such remarkable remains.

In the following pages Pat Wastell Norris answers the questions about "who?" and "why?" with gratifying completeness, and also confirms all suspicions about remarkable goings-on. It turns out that the rough-sawn mini-metropolis was built by her father, Fred Wastell, who needed something to do after the Great Depression interrupted his rather genteel existence as the son of a well-bred factory manager in nearby Alert Bay. Pat grew up there in a world of kelp dolls and killer whales with her younger sister and a very odd assortment of millworkers, coastal drifters and well-bred relatives, who good-humouredly rolled up their sleeves and learned some very un-genteel survival skills. Remarkable events, ranging from her aging grandmother's mastery of gasboat handling to her mother's emergency medical heroics, performed aboard storm-tossed towboats on battered loggers and expectant mothers, were a daily occurrence.

Pat Norris' memoir of growing up wet does more than fill the intriguing blank left in BC Coast history under the name of Telegraph Cove; it provides us with one of the more charming and insightful portraits we have yet had of upcoast life between the wars, a busy and colourful period justifiably described as the golden age of the BC coast.

Howard White

TELEGRAPH COVE

The brochure contained several beautiful photos of the BC coast and a description of the charter trips that were offered. One of them was a sail up the coast to the Indian village of Mamalilaculla. This village, it stated accurately, had been deserted for many years but it had now been reclaimed by descendants of its original inhabitants and was prepared to welcome visitors. The trip offered, the brochure went on, "an incomparable opportunity to interface with the Indians."

"Oh my god," I thought, "what would father have made of this!"

My father interfaced with the Indians every day of his life and with a lot of other coastal inhabitants too, and you can bet that his experiences were very different from the sanitized version of real life being offered to these earnest Tilley-hatted tourists. There was the time, for example, that he made every effort to interface with at least one Indian at Kingcome and all that turned up was a couple of starving dogs—but I'm getting ahead of myself.

It was my grandfather who named it Telegraph Cove. When he arrived in Alert Bay in 1909, Vancouver Island's north coast lay silent and virtually empty—its scattering of inhabitants were Indian tribes in their villages and a handful of white people. In 1912 the staccato click of a telegraph key and the faint crackle of a bad telephone line penetrated that silence to some slight degree when the federal government completed a telephone-telegraph line from Campbell River to northern Vancouver Island. When J.T. Phalen, the Superintendent of Telegraphs, was looking for a suitable location for a lineman's station close to Alert Bay, my grandfather suggested a little cove where the lineman's boat could be safely moored. Since it now needed to be properly identified, my grandfather promptly added place-naming to his services and called it Telegraph Cove.

And so, in 1912, telegraph lineman Bobby Cullerne became the Cove's first inhabitant. He lived in a one-room shed-roofed structure that, in a different guise, is still there. He not only lived alone, he worked alone; the telegraph line was simply strung from tree to tree along the shoreline and he patrolled the shore in his boat. His job required some rudimentary domestic skills, some familiarity with the internal combustion engine, a certain degree of seamanship and the ability to climb trees rather than telephone poles.

Apart from his government salary, Bobby's circumstances were no different from anyone else's in the vicinity. His life, like theirs, demanded strength of character, capability, versatility—and a sense of humour. The coast was not for the frivolous or the irresponsible. Lost in its immensity, unable to communicate with their fellows, cut off from the conveniences of the city, its people were do-it-yourselfers to a man/woman/child. They had common sense which served them better than intellectual brilliance—and they worked nonstop. In one sense, they lived a life of privilege, for they had the luxury of a pristine environment. Unfortunately it was a luxury they failed to recognize, for aesthetic appreciation pre-supposes leisure—and leisure was in short supply. Despite their best efforts, a lot of them died because their occupations were dangerous and nature, itself, is merciless.

A frontier offers opportunity to the entrepreneur and independence to the self-sufficient. And so it was possible for my father, dispossessed by the Great Depression, to start a business and, of necessity, a community at Telegraph Cove. He brought his bride there and that's where my sister and I, their two daughters, grew up. As a result we had an unconventional—and vastly entertaining—upbringing.

Not in his wildest dreams, however, could my father have envisioned what was to come. When my grandparents' picnics at deserted Indian villages were rained out, my grandmother and her friends played bridge on a wooden box in one of the longhouses. My father wouldn't have believed that, just a few decades later, boatloads of people would devote considerable time and money to glimpse a reconstructed Indian culture. And for my father, a boat was a means of earning a livelihood. He had the best one he could afford and kept it well maintained—for one day our lives might depend on it. Kayakers, paddling around in their cockleshells with no purpose other than the enjoyment of nature, he considered damn fools. As for whale-watchers, when Bill Mackay proposed a business based on this activity, my father felt compelled to disabuse him of his naiveté. "Bill," he said, "nobody's going to come up here to look at Blackfish."

He was wrong, but understandably so, for the early days were different—very different—from those that followed.

THE WILD WEST (COAST)

I

Alert Bay – This settlement, on the southern side of Cormorant Island, is on the northeastern side of Broughton Strait opposite the mouth of the Nimpkish River. In addition to being a commercial fishing port, it is a distributing centre for the many logging communities in the outlying districts.

British Columbia Pilot

His name was Alfred Marmaduke Wastell, which says it all. He was a typical English gentleman with all the strengths and weaknesses that the term implies—and he was my grandfather. He was immaculate in his dress and tolerant and whimsical in his outlook, and how he ever came to be the manager of anything as down-to-earth as a box factory is difficult to imagine, since no one else in his large family ever seems to have engaged in any practical activity. But that's exactly what he was—the manager of a fish processor's box factory in Alert Bay, a little community on the British Columbia coast some two hundred miles north of Vancouver. When he arrived there in 1909, it had exactly nineteen white inhabitants and about two hundred native Indian ones; it was, essentially, a Kwakiutl village.

My grandfather's parents and their growing family had originally lived on the south coast of England. Family documents describe my great-grandfather's occupation as "Gentleman." Spelled with a capital G, that simply meant that he didn't have to work for a living and could spend his days doing whatever suited his fancy. Somewhere along the line he fancied living in Canada, so he packed up the household and travelled to Ontario. He didn't emigrate, you understand; he didn't have to. The British Empire included all the pink bits on the globe and, as one of the largest pink bits, Canada was not an independent country but simply another part of the Empire.

The family settled in Haliburton, Ontario where my grandfather Duke, the last in a family of ten, was born. To me the words "ten children" and "nervous

breakdown" occur simultaneously, but that wasn't the case with the Wastells. They had a big house, plenty of "help," and a laid-back attitude. My grandfather remembered a happy and rambunctious childhood of sliding down the staircase on a metal tea tray and being held by the heels down the well by an Irish maid as punishment for some mischief. His father, however, was middle-aged when my grandfather was born and, as he got older, he grew nostalgic for his native land and decided to move his family back to England.

As the youngest in the family, my grandfather had never known England. Canada was *his* native land; he was no longer a child and he had had all the education he was going to get. He resolved to stay where he was, and went out and got himself a job "licking stamps," as he put it, at a local lumber mill. He was an agreeable and conscientious employee, and before long he began to learn the box-making business. He began, as well, to squire around the local young ladies, one of whom was Mary Elizabeth Sharpe.

Mame, as she was called, was the daughter of a Great Lakes captain who was away on his ship most of the time. Her mother, worn out by the birth of seven children, was in ill health. With an absentee father and an ailing mother, much of the household management fell to Mame, who was the eldest, and this experience shaped her personality. She became immensely capable and hard-working—and she became used to running the show. She was left, as well, with a marked distaste for large families in general and babies in particular.

By 1897, Mame and Duke had known each

other for five years, during which time she had flirted with many others, but he had remained constant in his affection. The choice of a mate is so often dictated by unspoken—if not unconscious—motives. That was the case here. My grandfather knew, by then, that Mame possessed the practicality and common-sense that he needed. She, in turn, was sure by this time that Duke would be a more considerate and devoted husband than her father had been to her mother. Once they had decided to marry, my grandfather wrote a touching letter to his future father-in-law which said, in part:

Should you think it proper to accept me as a son-in-law, I will forever do my utmost to make Mame happy and make you feel that you have not misplaced your trust and that you have placed the future of your daughter with one who will love and cherish her and that you may rest without the least thought of her being unhappy or neglected.

He was accepted, of course. The only difficulty was the distance that now separated them. My grandfather, by then established in his career in the box-making industry, was working for Barnet Sawmills on the west coast. So my grandmother said good-bye to her family and the big house on the shore of Lake Ontario and made the long train journey to New Westminster where they were married.

Almost immediately, my grandfather's devotion was put to the test. It had been a bleak little wedding with no friends or family present, and after only a few months in New Westminster my grandmother was overcome by homesickness. She missed canoeing on Lake Ontario, she missed the muskmelons that grew there, and most of all she missed her family. And so her husband, as good as his promise to make her happy, left his job. The two packed their household possessions in big wooden boxes and made the journey back to Ontario.

My grandfather found another job there and then his devotion was *really* put to the test. Mame, having tasted the wild west, decided that the east was stuffy and tiresome and that she much preferred British Columbia. Once again, my grandfather quit his job; once again, they packed the wooden boxes and left for New Westminster. Here, my grandmother's indecision ended. The west was now her life and she never saw Ontario again. She did, however, see her family; eventually all of them came west to live.

My father Fred was born in New Westminster a year or two after his mother had finally decided where she wanted to live. They weren't settled yet, however, for when he was nine, the BC Fishing and Packing Company, a fish processing company, offered my grandfather the job of managing the box factory it had recently acquired at Alert Bay. The enterprise had been badly managed, but its new owners felt that, given a year, my grandfather could get it running properly. This is what they proposed to him.

The whole family responded to the idea with

The BC Fishing and Packing Company's box factory crew at Alert Bay. My grandfather, Duke Wastell, at left.

The BC Fishing and Packing Company's box factory at Alert Bay.

enthusiasm. For Duke, it was a professional challenge; for Mame, who had finally cut her emotional ties to Ontario, it promised two activities that she especially enjoyed: boating and bathing, as it was then called. For my nine-year-old father Fred, it promised an adventure straight out of the *Boy's Own Annual*—an Indian village!

So late one Vancouver evening, the three Wastells embarked on a Union steamship. While they slept, the ship pushed northward up Georgia Strait, paused for slack water and then proceeded through Seymour Narrows and on into Johnstone Strait. By noon the next day, they had reached Alert Bay, a wide crescent-shaped bay that stretched along the southern shore of Cormorant Island. All along the bay, a broad pebble beach ran down to the water, and behind it lay the dense coastal forest. Following the shoreline, between the beach and the trees, stood a string of buildings: assorted frame houses, a small church with elaborate white gingerbread trim, the blank faces of huge Indian long-houses staring out from behind towering totem poles, and finally, the buildings and wharves that marked the box factory and the fish cannery. The ship docked at the cannery wharf, the gangway was lowered into place, and the Wastells disembarked to join a world that, unbeknownst to them, was to be their home not for a

year, but for the rest of their lives.

My grandfather busied himself with the problems of the box factory, while around him the community of Alert Bay changed and grew. The original white inhabitants—a handful of missionaries and fishing company employees—were joined by the operators of a new government wireless station, by a doctor and nurses who worked in the mission hospital, by oil company employees who provided marine fuel services, by teachers for the expanding school, and by government forest and fisheries wardens. Even with all the new arrivals, it remained a small community. All its white inhabitants had originally been city people whose jobs had required them to come to Alert Bay. Once there, they tried to approximate life in the city as closely as possible. They were what was then termed "respectable" people, an appellation that differentiated them from the non-respectable loggers who surrounded and out-numbered them, and who weren't considered respectable mainly because they were drunk all the time. They were drunk all the time because they did physically exhausting, deadly dangerous work and lived in isolation in camps that were lost in the vast coastal wilderness. Consequently, it was hardly surprising that whenever a logger received payment for a boom of logs that had been sent to "town"—Vancouver or

New Westminster—his friends gathered round in the nearest beer parlour for a little celebration.

As the liquor flowed, these parties got strenuous. At one of them, someone with a new pair of caulk boots initiated a contest. Caulk boots are high-laced leather footgear, as stiff and heavy as ski boots, and like ski boots, they give their wearers a clumping gait. It's the soles of the boots, however, that make them indispensable in the woods. Protruding from the thick leather are dozens of razor-sharp nails that allow the wearer to cling like a fly to the rounded and unstable surface of a log. In this competition, each man in turn put on the new boots and tried to see how far he could run up the wall. Those who failed to let go quickly enough when they had reached the limit of their ascent fell off, landing on their heads rather than on their feet, thereby losing the game and having to buy drinks all around.

Fortunately, the walls were lined with boards but as this activity didn't do much to improve their appearance and as he feared further damage to his property the proprietor, Charlie Cavanaugh, resorted to the lame excuse that he was obliged to shut down the bar because his liquor supply had run out. He fooled no one. The loggers decided that if he couldn't keep a more abundant supply of liquor on hand, the hotel wasn't worthy of the name and had better be dumped into the sea. Since the building lay on the edge of a big, flat table of rock almost overhanging the water, this procedure posed no particular problem for a gang of loggers. Each man went to his boat and brought back his pump jack, a piece of equipment usually used to extricate logs from tangled slopes and send them down into the water below. They set the jacks under the shore side of the building and commenced to raise it off its foundations. It wasn't long before the hotel started to creak and groan, and Charlie, by now aware that all was not as it should be, went out to investigate. What he saw convinced him that he'd better go inside and "find" some more liquid refreshment.

The crew of the Union steamship *Cassiar* was more successful at closing the bar and making it stick. Gerald Rushton, in his book *Whistle Up The Inlet* says:

Stories about the roistering aboard the SS Cassiar *were not exaggerated in the days when hand-logging was at its peak. The vessel's bar did a roaring trade, particularly when loggers headed for the city with a season's earnings after camp was paid off. Frequently, the master would have to order the bar closed, and it sometimes took two husky mates to restore order.*

SS *Cassiar*

My grandmother (standing in Panama hat), my grandfather (wearing spats), and three young guests on the newly launched *Klinekwa*—so newly launched that her mast has not been stepped (c.1912).

My grandfather's lifetime consumption of alcohol didn't exceed a couple of glasses of sherry, but he was tolerant and practical when it came to the drinking habits of others. This was just as well since, by 1912, he was not only the mill manager, but the local Justice of the Peace.

One weekend, the Provincial Police at Alert Bay consulted with him in his latter capacity. They had received a message from Minstrel Island concerning an attempted murder, and they wanted my grandfather to accompany them to the scene in order to lay charges, or do whatever a Justice of the Peace was required to do under the circumstances.

So, on a particularly beautiful Sunday morning, some eight hours after the reported incident, they set off in the police boat for Minstrel Island. The first thing they noticed upon their arrival was a dozen or so loggers sleeping on the sun-warmed rocks beside the hotel. Questioning revealed that the hotel's owner had gone to Vancouver and left his wife and, in my grandfather's words, "a little sawed-off cook" to look after the premises. Once they were roused from their sleep, the loggers readily acknowledged that on the previous night they had had a little party. Their powers of recall ranged from hazy to nil but they did agree that, once again, an unscheduled bar closure had caused all the trouble.

"That little runt who was tending the bar decided that we'd had too much," said one of the group, "and he told the boss's wife that they had better close up till we sobered up a bit."

The management did just that, which was a mistake because one of the boys went down to his boat and got a boom auger, an instrument used to bore four-inch holes in boomsticks—the long, straight logs that frame a log boom. He proceeded to bore a hole in the barroom door so that he could pull back the bolt that was locking it. When the two people inside voiced their displeasure over this turn of events, the loggers proposed draping a boomchain over the cook's shoulders and throwing him into the chuck. At this point the owner's wife fled to get a message to the police.

Having heard the evidence, the Justice of the Peace assembled all those involved, thrashed the matter out, and fined the boom auger expert ten dollars—with an order to replace the barroom door.

About the only other entertainment the loggers had were the dances at this same Minstrel Island. They were dances in name only for, probably because of the acute shortage of females, they invariably deteriorated into fist-fights and ended up as fully fledged brawls. The best you could say for them was that they were a change from logging.

It was understandable, then, that the "respectable" people felt it necessary to maintain their standards. But that didn't mean that they were stuffy or intolerant. Quite the reverse. Life on the coast fostered a sense of permanent irreverence. Knowing intimately so many diverse characters made us very aware of the sterling qualities of those with no pretensions, and forever impatient with snobbishness and self-importance.

Ten years after his arrival in Alert Bay, my father was off to the University of British Columbia, the temporary terms of my grandfather's employment were long forgotten, and the decade of the 1920s was about to begin.

The Roaring Twenties bowled through North America, bringing the message that prosperity and pleasure were out there for everyone. Overnight, the wind-up Victrolas changed their tune. The refined squealing of Galli-Curci was replaced by a tinny voice warbling, "You scream, I scream, we all scream for ice cream."

The young, the affluent, the sophisticated, the urban, all got the message first but it wasn't long before sober citizens began to get that fun feeling as well. Small business owners, people whose lives had been an unremitting struggle to collect their modest receivables, now exulted because their years of thrift had provided them with nest eggs and their success in the stock market had turned those nest eggs into portfolios that would ensure them not only comfortable retirement, but luxury. And since the bonhomie that comes with prosperity can't be contained, it rolled on without a pause into the furthest reaches of BC.

My father and his parents were perfectly positioned to enjoy the new decade. The company supplied them with a large comfortable house surrounded by a pretty garden and a tennis court. It also supplied the services of a Chinese cook. Their circumstances were made even more pleasant by the fact that they now owned a little yacht, the *Klinekwa*. Each summer she was meticulously scraped and varnished and otherwise prepared for a season of picnics and overnight jaunts. And when my father returned from university, he brought his car, a 490 Chevrolet, back with him on the coastal steamer. Since the community had no real roads, he and his friends piled in, cranked the engine into life and racketed

Chong with a kitchen knife and Alex MacDonald with an unidentified object, (c.1919) Alert Bay.

Pretty girls and handsome young men, c. 1915. The girl on the right is Mary Easthope of the Easthope engine family. She later married Alex Macdonald.

around the mill yard.

Winter and summer, my grandparents' house overflowed with guests. They had the wherewithal and the inclination for a lively social life, and my father—handsome and full of fun—was the belle of this ball. Yet, when Fred Wastell finally became engaged, it was not to one of the carefree flirts that surrounded him, but to Emma McCoskrie, an earnest young nurse who had come to work in the local hospital.

Emma's upbringing could not have been more different from Fred's. Whereas he had been an indulged and adored only child, encouraged to have as much fun as possible, she had lost her mother at the age of three and, bewildered and lonely, had been sent to live in the joyless household of a childless aunt and uncle.

Now, however, she was the fiancee of the local "catch." She had, in Mame, a domineering and slightly jealous future mother-in-law and, in Duke, a gentle and welcoming future father-in-law, and for

the first time in her life she found herself part of a jovial household dedicated to good times. Friends and relatives, missionaries and businessmen, middle-aged bridge players, and young teachers and nurses all enjoyed the hospitality and high spirits of my grandparents' home. Old photos show civilized life in the foreground and untamed wilderness in the background. Here they sit, stand or lounge, pretty girls with smart haircuts and chic country clothes; handsome young men with crinkly, sexy smiles wearing white flannels and clutching tennis rackets. In the garden in front of the honeysuckle stands Chong, the cook, resplendent in starched white. My grandmother poses serenely on the deck of the *Klinekwa* wearing a finely striped cotton dress with a big white collar, and a deep-crowned straw hat trimmed with a band of fabric that matches her dress.

Ten years of economic depression and another six of war were about to obliterate all traces of that pleasant life—and it all began in 1928.

My grandmother and my father, seated, Chong in his off-duty cap and three of the ever-present guests (c.1912).

II

TELEGRAPH COVE MILLS LTD

Telegraph Cove is on the eastern side of Beaver Cove about $3\frac{1}{2}$ cables southwestward of Ella Point. It is a small cove extending about $1\frac{1}{2}$ cables in a southeasterly direction, with a width of approximately 200 feet at its narrowest point.

The Broughton Lumber and Trading Company's wharf, the face of which is about 170 feet long, has depths from 17 to 22 feet. The local steamer calls regularly. There is a sawmill, store and post office, connected to the general telephone system. Diesel oil, gasoline and water are procurable for small vessels.

This cove provides excellent shelter for small craft in all weathers.

British Columbia Pilot

In 1928, the BC Fishing and Packing Company switched from wooden boxes to corrugated cardboard. Their need for lumber was gone; within weeks, the box factory was closed and within months its assets—including the manager's house—were disposed of. Chong, the cook, like the manager and the other forty company employees, was dismissed.

In 1928, there were no severance packages, no unemployment insurance cheques, no pension plans to roll into an RRSP. My grandfather was nearing sixty, not the most employable age. He was a man however, of limitless equanimity. He responded to this sudden change in fortune by withdrawing a sizeable sum from his bank account, buying a transcontinental train ticket, and booking passage to England on the brand new Cunard ship, the *Queen Mary*. There he would spend several months relaxing and visiting family. He brought home a beautiful souvenir book containing blueprints and full page water-colour paintings of the interior of this vast new ship and, as a child, I spent hours lying on my grandparents' green carpet poring over these illustrations. Having spent my life, to that point, in a rugged and remote world, I was both puzzled and entranced by the grandeur depicted between its handsome blue and gold covers.

My grandmother had not been aware of these travel plans until her husband announced them one morning, at breakfast.

"Well then, Mame," Duke said, "how would you like to pack your valise and take a trip to England with me?"

My grandmother was astounded. *"England?"*

"Yes," said my grandfather. "Now that I'm no longer working we have the time to take a little holiday."

"I think that since you're not working it would be a lot more sensible for us to stay at home and save our money," said Mame.

"Oh, it won't be an expensive trip. We can stay with the family. They have plenty of room."

"I'd go mad sitting around all day with those people," she said. "Useless lot. Perfectly able-bodied people spending their days doing absolutely nothing."

"They don't sit around all day," he protested mildly. "They go out in the garden. They play croquet. Father even has his Peterborough canoe," he added. "Takes it out on the pond every day. You could go canoeing."

My grandmother was not to be enticed. "You go if you want to."

And so he did, while she stayed in Alert Bay and began to adjust to life without a cook, a tennis court—or a salary.

It was now that Mame supplied her contribution to the marriage. Duke's parents, having been spared the necessity of earning a living, had consequently imbued their children with a lofty disregard for money. As a result, my grandfather had a tenuous grasp of the financial facts of life and a dangerous attraction to mining stocks. Mame's upbringing, on the other hand, had made her the *de facto* head of a large family, and had indelibly impressed upon her consciousness the value of a dollar. Early in her marriage, she had realized that she must wrest away as much of my grandfather's discretionary income as possible, lest his financial follies bankrupt them. She had invested this little hoard in mortgages and rental real estate, the returns from which kept them both for the rest of their lives.

My parents, meanwhile, were struggling with the problem of their own future. At the time of their wedding in June 1928 my father, (with fine disregard for charges of nepotism), was the bookkeeper for the same box factory that his father managed. He and Emma were married by a friend of the family in a lovely old church in Victoria. My mother wore a chic silk crêpe de chine dress that had been designed and made by a French dressmaker. They went to California for a leisurely honeymoon and, when they returned to Alert Bay, it was to a brand new house that had been built for them. But, within months, this well-ordered world fell down around their ears.

For a year after the box factory closed, my father was retained to close the books and finalize the business there, but in the fall of 1929 another disturbing event took place. Three thousand miles away the New York stock market crashed and the shock waves travelled all the way from the east to the west. Jobs disappeared overnight.

My father would say later that it wasn't a great start for a family that now included an infant daughter. But he failed to mention that the BC Fishing and Packing Company had offered him employment in their Vancouver offices; I don't think he ever even considered this an option. From the moment he stepped off the coastal steamer with his parents at the age of nine, the coast was where he belonged. It was not an unreasonable view, for it was a boy's paradise, offering space, freedom and adventure. By the time he was a man of thirty, this way of life was so much a part of him that to relinquish it was simply not an alternative.

Instead, he turned his attention to a piece of land that my grandfather owned just down the coast: four hundred acres of waterfront that he had acquired as payment of a bad debt. Duke always played down the bad debt aspect, maintaining that the Royal Bank had urged him to buy out their stake in the property. I'm sure they did. They had been stung, too, and their fellow creditor no doubt seemed the likeliest prospect to buy them out. Mame, a much shrewder judge of character than her husband, would never have lent $1200 to such an obviously poor risk, and when the debtor predictably defaulted and signed over this chunk of wilderness instead, she was furious. As it turned out, her distress was unjustified.

Over the years my grandfather had taken timber off the property and, in the mid-1920s, he and a group of Japanese had built a salmon saltery and a primitive little mill there. My father had a financial interest in the mill—he had supplied the money for the machinery—but for the preceding two years it had lain idle. Now he proposed to resurrect this mill and make a living cutting lumber. He contacted his childhood friend in New Westminster, Alex MacDonald, and together they embarked on this new endeavour.

That the undertaking involved up-grading a sawmill that was then hardly worthy of the name, providing housing for themselves and a crew, setting up a water system and a generating plant—in fact establishing

June 1928. My mother wore a chic crêpe de chine dress. My father's best man was his future business partner, Alex Macdonald.

The bleak beginnings of Telegraph Cove Mills.

a town as well as a business, all on a shoestring, didn't seem to strike them as an insurmountable problem. Or perhaps it was my father's sanguine temperament that made it all seem feasible.

At any rate, it began to come together. My grandmother's brothers could build or fix anything, and they proceeded to do just that. Three Chinese, including Chong the cook, all former employees of the box factory, arrived unbidden, fixed up an old shack (forever after known as the China House) and presented themselves as crew members. Chong, still wearing his immaculate whites, became camp cook. They were joined by others. The going rate of pay was twenty-five cents an hour, although by this time, with the Depression grown even worse and without the cushion of unemployment insurance there were men willing to work for nothing more than room and board. That approach couldn't have struck the new company as a very professional arrangement, however, for they continued to pay wages.

That the great shortage of jobs could have tragic consequences was borne out by the experience of David, a young family friend who had just graduated from UBC with a bachelor of arts degree. Back then BAs were not the dime-a-dozen credentials they are today. They entitled the holder to teach at any public school and should have opened many other doors to employment. Now every one of those doors was tightly shut and, unwilling to live off his parents, David asked about a job at the mill. As sympathetic as he

was, Alex couldn't afford another crew member, but David finally got work in the big Wood & English mill at nearby Englewood. Unused to manual labour, he lasted three days before being killed while working on the green chain.

Telegraph Cove Mills, meanwhile, had acquired letterhead and business cards and a former seine boat, the *Mary W*, which was used for towing logs and delivering lumber. But towing logs and carrying lumber was not what she was designed for. This became apparent when, early on, they put an overly ambitious deck load on her and she nearly rolled over in a sea. She had defects as a towboat, too, for she was underpowered for the job.

Towing logs is a slow and tricky business. For one thing, the coast tides are strong and capricious. The tide out of Baronet Pass, for example, sweeps out of Blackney Pass and out around the east side of Malcolm Island. As the *Mary* emerged from Baronet Pass and rounded Cracroft Point, she had to pull sharply to port, almost doubling back in the direction from which she came in order to free herself from the tide's grip and get out into Johnstone Strait. A little more power would have made this manoeuvre unnecessary, but the *Mary* didn't have it. Then there was the wind. Johnstone Strait isn't the calmest body of water and any sizeable seas will tear a boom to pieces. Getting a boom in safely was always a combination of good luck and good management.

For the uninitiated, a log boom is a rectangle of

floating logs arranged side by side and end to end. Around their perimeter, boomsticks—extra long, extra straight logs secured end to end with great chunks of chain—maintain the rectangular shape. At regular intervals, lying at right angles to the logs and on top of them, are "swifters." They, too, are long straight logs fastened in place with boom chains; they give the boom stability and at the same time divide it into prescribed units called "sections."

To manoeuvre a boom out of a confined space, the tug keeps its unwieldy charge right alongside or pushes it bow-on, or both, until it's in open water. A cable "bridle" is attached to the two corners of one end of the rectangle, then the towline is attached to the bridle. Slowly, line is paid out, until the boom is far enough astern to be free of the negative effect of the wash from the tug's propeller. Then the towline is secured, and tug and tow are under way. Since towing, especially with a boat like the *Mary*, was a painfully slow business, my father made himself as comfortable as possible. He tipped back the high stool in the wheel-house, steered with his feet, and read *The Hiballer*, a modest trade publication for loggers which contained, among other things, a lot of dirty jokes.

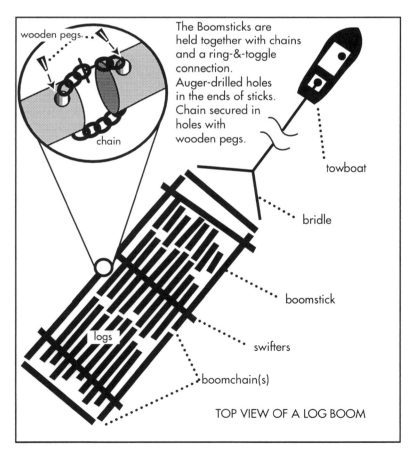

The Boomsticks are held together with chains and a ring-&-toggle connection. Auger-drilled holes in the ends of sticks. Chain secured in holes with wooden pegs.

wooden pegs

chain

towboat

bridle

boomstick

logs

swifters

boomchain(s)

TOP VIEW OF A LOG BOOM

That was on good days. But with no marine radio in existence, and therefore no accurate weather reports, there was only the barometer to warn of coming weather. So there were, inevitably, some bad days. There is no shelter in Johnstone Strait, and on rare occasions they were caught there by the weather. If conditions deteriorated quickly and unexpectedly, the boat and tow found themselves in exposed water and a rising wind. When the seas got to a certain height the logs, in their rectangle, would start to rise and fall, until finally one would catch on a boomstick. Its weight would hold the boomstick below the surface of the water, and now the other logs, like a herd of willful cattle, would surge, one by one, over the gap and into the open sea. Other escape routes would occur as logs washed over the boomsticks and the crew of the tug, looking astern, would see the boom disintegrating. By hauling in the towline and closing in on the boom it was sometimes possible to pry the logs off the boomsticks with a pike pole and salvage something of the tow. But if the weather was bad enough, the tow was lost and the financial repercussions, for a small sawmill like ours, were heartbreaking.

Nor did it take a storm to lose a boom; even the light chop caused by the clashing of wind and tide could do it, as happened one bright afternoon in Blackney Pass when the whirling tide met a brisk little westerly wind. A log bounced onto a boomstick and suddenly the boom was breaking up. The boat turned, manoeuvred into position alongside the boom, and the deck-hand, pike pole in hand, jumped down onto the logs. My father put the engine in neutral and hustled to the stern deck to hand him a line.

It didn't get that far. Instead there was one of those quick frightening moments that occur when huge inanimate objects wrestle control from their keeper and take charge. The boat and the boom, both in the grip of the tide, parted company. The towline caught a corner and pulled a fifty-foot boomstick up out of the water.

"Lifting *Jesus!*" yelled the deck-hand, fighting for balance.

My father sprinted for the wheel-house, the boat churned astern, and the towline strained along the log and finally

The *Klinekwa* scouting for logs among the maze of islands between Johnstone Strait and the Mainland, c. 1931.

snapped back into position. Some distance astern, the deck-hand, looking exceedingly lonely, bounced around on his little island of logs. He was rescued; the boom was not. In all directions the logs spun away with the tide, like truants out of school.

If, by some stretch of the imagination, these undertakings could have been considered adventures for the men, they were certainly adventures that my mother could have done without. With a year-old child she moved from her new house to a three-room shack perched on a bluff above the harbour. It had a wood stove, outdoor plumbing, and after some time, sporadic bursts of electricity from the newly installed but secondhand generating plant—a ten-horsepower Petters engine. Even when it was operating, this plant supplied only enough power for a few dim light bulbs. As a child, I was startled to learn how much illumination a light bulb could really give; it was as if I had been blind and then regained my sight. We were, it seems, like the *Mary,* perpetually underpowered!

The water supply came from a little creek that had been dammed and piped down to us through the woods. The pipe itself was buried underground to keep it from freezing, although it frequently did anyway, but there were other problems to contend with besides cold temperatures. When all danger of freezing was past, the bears came out. They were curious about the water gurgling underground and, with a couple of swipes, they would rip the pipe out of the

ground; the connections would break, and our water supply would dwindle and cease. In later years when plastic pipe replaced the original iron, it was even worse; they not only ripped it out, but chewed it before they were satisfied that it had no nutritional value.

Nor were these inconveniences repaid with a setting of great natural beauty. Instead the senses were assaulted from every side. The hills that sloped down to the small cove, today so lush and green and lovely, were then a sea of blackened stumps—the ravaged remains of logging and of a fire. Below the house, on the dock, the saltery still operated intermittently, filling the air with the stench of rotting fish guts, and forcing my mother to keep all the windows tightly closed.

There was no other English-speaking woman in the vicinity and the rain poured down unceasingly. To make matters worse, the first two winters that my parents spent there were unusually cold. Some perverse law of nature decrees that under such circumstances the weather will always try for a record. It did. The logs froze into a solid mass in the bay and so did the pipes under the flimsy house.

For Emma, then, the honeymoon ended abruptly in 1929. For Mame, the transition from her former life to this new one was easier because, for her, it carried some real psychological benefits. True, the lawn tennis parties were a thing of the past, she had pressing financial worries and she, herself, had replaced the Chinese cook in the kitchen and at the scrubbing board. But she and Duke were still living in the relative comfort of the more civilized community of Alert Bay, where they had moved into the house originally intended for my parents. They still had the *Klinekwa* and made frequent trips back and forth to keep in touch with the new enterprise at Telegraph Cove. And Mame was by nature frugal and resourceful. Most importantly, if doing meaningful tasks that confirm our worth in our society brings satisfaction, then she had that satisfaction in spades, for both she and the *Klinekwa* soon acquired a new career. Together, my

My mother in her trousseau finery en route to California by ship.

grandparents scouted the labyrinth of islands between the mainland and northern Vancouver Island on log-buying expeditions; in the days before radio telephone, the only way to find out which logging camps had booms to sell was to visit the camps themselves. It was an occupation that suited my grandmother perfectly. The daughter of a sea-captain, she loved being on the water and handled the boat with professional skill. She wore a neat, navy blue "afternoon dress" on these expeditions and did her grey hair up in a soft bun. In those pre-feminist days, the sight of this dignified figure running a boat with such assurance must have presented a puzzling picture. Docking smoothly at one logging camp, she rang "stop engines" and in the ensuing silence she was vastly amused to hear a logger on the log dump above her say to his companion, "Where in the world did that old lady come from?"

Not all their landings were so harmonious, however. Today's yachts tuck their powerful high-speed engines under the floorboards and run them with pilot-house controls. The *Klinekwa*'s big engine, with its huge iron clutch lever, required a spacious engine-room and an attendant with a strong arm. The engine-room was just aft of the pilot-house and its big windows gave a clear side view. Unfortunately this permitted my grandfather, who acted as engineer, to second-guess my grandmother, who acted as captain. As the boat approached a dock, Mame rang one bell as a signal to disengage the clutch. The engine did not respond. Leaning down through the engine-room door, my grandmother yelled, "Duke, I gave you one bell!"

There was no time for further conversation. The *Klinekwa* was, by this time, almost on top of the dock. My grandmother rang one bell and then two to put the engine full astern. The *Klinekwa* slid forward, still under way, and banged heavily against the piles.

While the lines were being secured there was silence but when the boat was safely tied up, Mame's frustration burst forth. "Duke, you old fool," she cried, "when I'm landing the boat, do what I say! I know what I'm doing. You can't see properly back there, so just answer the bells. If this keeps up, we're going to take someone's pilings out—and damage the little *Klinekwa.*" My grandmother considered the *Klinekwa* a member of the family and, as such, the boat had her deep affection—and her protection.

"Yes, yes, dear girl," said my grandfather. He never argued. There was no point in arguing because he knew what my grandmother did not: that men were always right, anyway.

The area of the north coast that they covered, the part within feasible towing distance of the mill, has neither the oppressive grandeur of the deep inlets to the east nor the exposed water of Johnstone Strait to the west. Instead, it is a maze of islands, large and small, scattered like the pieces of a jig-saw puzzle, their convoluted shapes forming endless waterways.

As a child of four I went along on many of their voyages. My mother, by now expecting my sister Bea, was no doubt delighted to have a brief respite from my company. And so we three wended our way down narrow channels, skirting kelp beds, checking the charts and consulting the tide book, as the *Klinekwa* slipped past mile after mile of impenetrable coastal forest. In those days—the days before bulldozers and heavy equipment—the pristine green wilderness seemed impregnable, for man had only nibbled at its edges.

The great trees crowded down to the high water mark, their branches dripping with Spanish moss. Around us bobbed the sea birds; eighty feet above us in the spiked tops of the cedars, bald eagles sat stern and alert. Occasionally, a mink streaked across the rocks where our wake, rolling out from the bows, bounced against the shoreline. Before us the water lay as pliant and lustrous as satin, and behind us our wake formed two ribbons of white lace.

It was only when we reached our destination that the spell was broken. Rounding one last point, we would come upon a cluster of floats tied to the shore, on them a few weather-beaten buildings, smoke rising from tin chimneys. There was the A-frame and the donkey engine, the latter protected from the unending rain by a patched corrugated iron roof. There was a hillside of logging slash, and in the water floated half-made-up booms of huge logs.

The people we met on these expeditions were an odd mixture. The coast has always mirrored the times.

From the very beginning I loved boats with a passion.

In the 1970s and 1980s it harboured, in its green recesses, not only loggers and fishermen but marine biologists studying whales, Viet Nam War veterans recovering from their horrors, and drug dealers posing as back-to-the-landers. In the 1930s besides the loggers and fishermen there were missionaries, remittance men and genuine back-to-the-landers.

The back-to-the-landers were, even amongst themselves, a disparate group. There were, for example, the Hallidays, who had a large farm in the remote reaches of Kingcome Inlet. They raised cattle, and in the "early" days they had *rowed* their produce the sixty

A summer outing on the *Klinekwa*, c. 1925. The man standing is my grandmother's brother Fred—one of my father's talented uncles.

miles to the nearest market in Alert Bay—a four day return trip. The very thought of rowing a heavily laden skiff thirty miles a day beggars the imagination. Against tides and winds, it must have been an unbelievably laborious undertaking. By the thirties they were making the journey by gasboat, but Salo, a Finn who had a homestead on Malcolm Island, still rowed to Alert Bay once a week to sell his butter and cream door-to-door. Granted, the return journey was more like five miles than sixty, for he rowed his big dory from Malcolm Island to the east side of Cormorant Island, secured it there and then hiked across the island to the settlement with his produce on his back. Nonetheless the trip must have required not only stamina but timing, for he needed a fair tide on both legs of his trip. No row boat is a match for the tides that race through those waters.

In an idyllic little bay on Pearse Island lived an English couple, the Youngs. They were a tiny little pair who grew daffodils as a cash crop. The fact that in the 1930s there was virtually no ready market for daffodils in that part of BC didn't seem to have occurred to them. Although their vegetable garden and the fish at their doorstep kept them from starving, theirs was a meagre existence. Yet they stayed there, I suppose because of financial constraints, until the end of their lives; long after they were gone, the daffodils bloomed each spring; a sudden sweep of gold in an otherwise unremittingly green landscape.

In contrast to the Youngs, who were unfailingly pleasant and polite, there lived, up in the then-inaccessible reaches of the Nimpkish River, a scowling German always referred to as "old Schalling." He appeared only rarely, rowing his dory on some private errand. It was reported that he had a wife, and even children, but no one seemed to have actually seen them. It was said, too, that someone, perhaps a timber cruiser, had inadvertently stumbled on his homestead one day and was greeted by Schalling brandishing a rifle and ordering him off. Certainly my mother, when she was still nursing in the local hospital, had a memorable encounter with him. He had appeared at the hospital one day, taciturn as ever, with a blood-soaked rag around one hand. When it was removed, it was discovered that he had lost two fingers in some kind of an accident. Somehow he had managed to row himself to the hospital from his remote homestead without bleeding to death en route. Even then, my mother swore, he did not seem in any particular distress. She had remained awed by such stoicism.

Each spring, when wild lilies bloomed in profusion in the meadows at the mouth of the Nimpkish River, we took the boat there for a picnic. We returned home with armfuls of the delicate mauve flowers; but all afternoon, as we picked them, I kept one eye out for Schalling—expecting him to appear from the depths of the forest like the gnomes in my books of fairy tales.

Although at four I was too young to appreciate it, I realize now that the greatest possible contrast in the human condition occurred in the relatively short distance between Soderman's Camp—wherever it happened to be at the moment—and the Indian village of Mamalilaculla on Village Island. We bought a lot of logs from Oscar Soderman, a tall bony Norwegian in his mid-fifties who had a peculiar claim to fame. He had married, whether while under the influence or in full possession of his faculties we could never be quite sure, a former Madam who now ran the camp—and Oscar—with an iron hand. Sidney Soderman was reported to be a holy terror of a boss, and loggers are not easily intimidated. The only indication we ever got of this came one day when my father and Sidney were conferring about logs. There was a knock at the door and Sidney yelled, "Who is it?"

"It's Bob," came the reply.

"Well bob the hell out of there", shouted Sidney, and there was the sound of rapidly retreating steps.

On my grandparent's visits, however, Sidney was always hospitality itself. If we arrived anywhere near a meal hour, we were always invited to join Oscar and her in the cookhouse; and while Oscar and my grandfather discussed how much timber was in the water, what species it was and when the log scaler would be around, my grandmother and Sidney Soderman had their own conversation. Although Mame was the soul of rectitude, she and Sidney seemed to get along fine;

perhaps each recognized in the other a strong character and a good business sense.

Two very different women lived a few miles away at Mamalilaculla. The Misses O'Brien and Dibben shared a little frame house above a white clamshell beach, the only white people in the village. These two spinster ladies had left England, their families and everything familiar, and had travelled across the Atlantic, across the continent and up the BC coast to this isolated Indian village. They were Anglican missionaries, sent on this bizarre journey as others of their kind were shipped off to darkest Africa.

Miss O'Brien had a small private income which she used to build a church, a school and a small sanatorium for tuberculosis patients. In theory this was a perfect example of practical Christianity; in practice it didn't fly, though certainly not for lack of devotion on the part of the ladies. Since the Indians already had their own rich spiritual heritage and few of the young were terribly anxious to be educated—and since the men, in particular, were disinclined to pay any attention to women—the project was not a howling success. Nonetheless, the two missionaries continued their endeavours for the remainder of their lives, and the Indians came to realize that their presence had its advantages. They could always earn a small but

In the early days, the saltery was still operating and in season the warehouses were stacked floor to ceiling with huge boxes of salted salmon.

dependable cash income from chopping the ladies' wood and delivering their mail and provisions from the nearest settlement at Echo Bay.

Since the Misses O'Brien and Dibben had no logs to sell, our visits to them were purely social in nature and were, in fact, opportunities to check on their welfare. It was usually afternoon by the time we reached Village Island and the ladies always invited us into their untidy little sitting-room for tea. I was given an atlas or something of the kind to look at while the adults chatted. What they talked about is hard to imagine, for the two women had no radio, no current reading matter, and no regular contact with other white people. Yet the social niceties seem not to have been impaired.

One day, for some long-forgotten reason, my grandmother and my father and I made the long trip to Halliday's farm at the head of Kingcome Inlet. It proved a memorable experience for me; it introduced me to an enormous beast called a cow. I had seen any number of wild creatures but I had never seen any farm animals, nor had I ever seen a farm. In fact, I had never seen a field, and I found the huge, flat expanse of grass most unusual.

We went into the barn where my father and Mr. Halliday got into an interminable conversation. Fascinated by the huge animals that surrounded us, I could finally stand it no longer. I approached a tan-coloured cow very cautiously and stretched out one finger. I didn't know I was being observed until we were on our way back to the boat.

"Well, what did the cow feel like?" asked my father.

I considered. "It was soft and warm," I said.

My grandmother, meanwhile, had made her own discovery. It must be explained here that Mame was not a passive participant in the game of life. She was ever alert to opportunities and took full advantage of those that presented themselves. Typically, she had found an opportunity at Halliday's farm.

"Fred," she said, indicated a large cardboard carton, "will you put that box on the boat. It's going to the Bay with us."

"What's in it?" asked my father.

"Frogs," said my grandmother.

"*Frogs?*"

"For the garden," she explained. "Frogs are wonderful for eating bugs, and this place is just alive with them. The Halliday boys have caught me a box full."

Under her direction, he put the box on the back deck where the frogs would get plenty of fresh air, and we headed homeward down Kingcome Inlet. Before long, it began to blow hard. The boat started to lunge and roll, and when my grandmother went to check her charges on the back deck she was distressed to find that the box had fallen over. She hurried to the wheel-house.

"Fred," she said, "those frogs are getting out of their box."

"That's very unfortunate," said my father, "for the frogs."

"Don't joke," said Mame, "I want you to go out and get them back in the box."

When it came to his mother, whom he called Elizabeth, my father was endlessly forbearing. He handed her the wheel and headed for the stern. I followed him as far as the galley where a window gave a view of the deck.

By now, frogs were flying in all directions. A frog is probably constitutionally constructed to land on a level surface. On the back deck, there were no level surfaces. There weren't even any stationary ones. Consequently, the frogs had become disoriented. They were leaping into the sea, rolling around in the scuppers, and clinging precariously to coils of rope and the winch. My father and the frogs proceeded to leap around the back deck with mad abandon, my father somewhat disadvantaged by the fact that he was laughing uncontrollably. Glued to the window, I watched the proceedings which, for amusement value, certainly exceeded anything the Muppets could have produced. Eventually, my father did get some of the frogs back into their box and they were duly released into my grandparents' garden. Today some of their descendants must still live in the marshy spots on Cormorant Island.

The boat that took us on all these journeys was thirty-five feet long. She had graceful lines, comfortable accommodation and a heavy-duty Atlas Imperial gas engine. Nothing like that engine exists today. It pushed her along at the remarkable speed of ten knots, hence her name *Klinekwa* which means "lightning" in the Kwakiutl language. The Atlas had two big cast-iron cylinders painted bright engine-enamel green, and it threw a thirty-inch flywheel. Once the engine was started by hand-cranking, the igniters were adjusted manually until the engine was running smoothly. It ran with a resounding "tha-thunk," "tha-thunk," "tha-thunk," that could be heard for miles across the water. There was a gas tank with a glass gauge on the wall of the engine-room, and gas was pumped by hand from the large tank in the hull into this smaller, gravity-fed one.

On one log-buying trip, my grandfather went into the engine-room to check the gas level and found, to his considerable agitation, a thin stream of gas spraying out of a pinhole in the tank. As it sprayed out and mixed with air, it turned the engine-room into one huge carburetor. The mix cannot have been just right, however, for as yet it hadn't demonstrated the principles of the internal combustion engine. Instinctively, Duke put his finger over the hole. His finger continued right on through the wall of the tank. He shoved his handkerchief in the now gaping hole and stopped the engine. Mame, who was in the wheelhouse steering, was startled by the sudden loss of power.

"Duke, what in the world are you doing?" she said, peering down the steps that let from the pilot-house to the engine-room.

"We have a little problem with the gas tank," he said, gesturing at his handkerchief, now sodden with gas.

"Mercy on us," she said.

"I'm going to have to stop this up with something," said Duke. "You keep an eye on the boat while I see what I can find for a patch."

Mame headed back to the pilot-house.

"If she gets near the rocks, call me," he said, "and we'll push her off with the pike pole."

So while they drifted, my grandfather made a more substantial patch from some gasket material, a piece of tin, and a great deal of electrician's tape. At my grandmother's suggestion they "aired out" the engine-room. And then my grandfather warily started the engine once again, and they "tha-thunked" home with only a small drip of gas forming

My father Fred Wastell, at about the time of his marriage.

now and again at the bottom of the tank.

Next day the tank was removed and placed on our dock, and a water hose was run into it. For twenty-four hours, water ran into one opening and out of the other, in preparation for a more permanent patch job. Meanwhile, a good piece of iron and some solder were assembled. At the first touch of the blowtorch, the tank exploded with an ear-shattering bang, showering hundreds of pieces of metal in all directions and scaring the hell out of the holder of the blowtorch. "That gas," said my father thoughtfully at dinner, "is amazing stuff."

The early days. The lineman's shack is on the left; below it the saltery and the warehouse for fish storage.

EDUCATION COMES IN MANY FORMS

The tidal streams in Blackney Passage are strong and attain a rate of 5 knots at times, with heavy races off Cracroft Point on both the flood and the ebb. Two portions of the flood, or east-going stream, flowing northward and southward, respectively, off Hanson Island, meet near the southern end of Blackney Passage causing a strong tidal race in mid channel.

British Columbia Pilot

Up to this point, all my adventures had been experienced not just as an only child but as *the* only child, for I had no playmates. However, I had parents and grandparents and knew everyone else that I encountered in my little world, and they all knew me. It was an entirely satisfactory existence as far as I was concerned. But parents can never leave well enough alone. Each summer my mother took me, and later my baby sister Bea, to Victoria, where she spent a month visiting relatives and getting some respite from her isolated life. All well and good, but on these holidays she always took great pains to introduce me to the sub-species called "children," an experience that I found to be an unremitting strain.

Frankly, children frightened me. I understood adults; they were logical and dependable. Children were unpredictable and, well, childish. As well, they travelled in huge groups of perhaps five or six. Then there was the culture gap; they were city and I was country. They took something called chalk and made marks on something called sidewalks and did something called hop-scotch. Sidewalks, in themselves, were a great source of wonderment to me. That ribbon of cement with the neat, regular divisions stretching in all directions as far as the eye could see was a puzzling phenomenon for someone who had only walked on a dock or along a trail through the woods.

By the time I was six, though, there were married members of the sawmill crew and, even in the country, there were other children of school age. Somehow we had to be educated. So in the summer of my sixth birthday, while in the city for her holiday, my mother arranged an appointment with the Superintendent of Education about our getting a local school.

The Superintendent of Education was formidably neat. He wore a navy serge suit that had been pressed, in some places, to a shine. On his big oak desk, small piles of paper lay in perfect alignment. In an anteroom a secretary typed busily, and in the street below cars passed. The Superintendent of Education gestured toward a chair and my mother sat down.

"You are...," he consulted his appointment book, "Mrs. Waistle."

"Wast*ell*," said my mother.

"And what can I do for you?" he asked.

"My husband has a little sawmill on the northern end of Vancouver Island," she said. "We have a small community there. I've come to see if we can get a school established for our children."

"And just where is it that you live?"

"Telegraph Cove," said my mother.

The Superintendent of Education consulted his maps and papers. It had taken him a lifetime of effort to reach his position and he was not a man to be trifled with. Looking at his maps, he decided that Mother was trying to do just that.

"There is already a local school in your area," he said. "There is, in fact, a one-room school approximately three miles away at Beaver Cove. The government would certainly not consider setting up another one. I happen to be of the opinion that it has never hurt a child to do a little walking. That's what feet are for." He smiled ever so slightly at his own wit.

Now it was my mother's turn to face the culture gap. How to replace this bureaucrat's vision of sturdy children trudging along a dusty country road, with something closer to reality. How to explain to a man with traffic streaming along outside his window that

29

in the woods behind our house the ground was steep and covered with rotting deadfalls. Under the fir and the hemlock and the cedar trees, salmonberry, devil's club and salal grew eight feet tall in dank darkness. The alternative to this jungle was the sea—often rough, always gurgling ominously with tide.

"The children can't walk to Beaver Cove," said my mother. "Nobody can walk to Beaver Cove. There's no road between the two communities."

"No road?" said the Superintendent of Education, puzzled.

"It's very rough country," said my mother. "Very

Jimmy painting the *Hili-Kum*'s mast. Our schoolhouse is the building directly beneath him with the three large windows.

steep. Straight down into the sea. The underbrush is terribly thick. Even if we managed to hack a trail through the woods, it wouldn't be safe for children."

The Superintendent of Education digested all this a bit at a time.

"I see," he said, more to himself than my mother. "I see."

"Well," he said finally, "I suppose in that case we could give you some assistance. We couldn't build a school in your community, of course, but if your company is prepared to supply a building and equip it, the government would supply a grant to pay a teacher's salary. You must understand," he added firmly, "that you will have to have a minimum of seven students to qualify for this grant."

"I'm sure we can meet those requirements," my mother said.

"Well that's settled, then," said the Superintendent of Education, rising and extending his hand. "Good-bye, Mrs. Waistle."

"Good-bye," said my mother.

The teacher's grant was duly processed. A side effect of the seven-children edict was the preference always given to job applicants with large families. My father had no intention of letting birth control endanger our government grant. And now everything else was up to us: the building, the furnishings, the school supplies and the maintenance.

There was a small house under construction at the mill at this time, and when my mother returned with her teacher's grant in hand, this building was modified slightly and became a school. The large front room became a classroom, and the three big windows that faced the stunning view were raised lest we students be distracted from the tasks at hand. There was a little covered porch for our coats and rubber boots, and behind the classroom there was a bedroom and a kitchen with one cold water tap. This was to be the teacher's accommodation. Outside there was a new privy with a brand new can of chloride of lime on the seat.

It's ironic that the next step, getting the furnishings and the equipment, was the easiest of all. We were far too isolated and too short of money to pursue these things in the conventional manner. But the Depression came to our aid. By then, it had ground on for six years, and the north coast was littered with evidence of its presence. In a nearby bay, there were the looming remains of a pulp mill that had never operated. The boilers for our mill had come from an abandoned coal mine. Everywhere, there were empty habitations left to the encroaching forest by disheartened owners. At Mitchell Bay on Malcolm Island, the population had shrunk to the point where the school had closed. We went over in the boat and found the abandoned schoolhouse. Inside, it was bright and hot and dusty. Someone had been into the building before us and had scattered books and papers on the floor, but everything we needed was there. The blackboards were removed from the walls, the desks unscrewed from the floor, the scattered books were carefully packed in cartons, and even the blackboard brushes were found in the grass outside and salvaged. We had our school.

But as yet we had no teacher. It was mid-September by now and once again things worked in our favour. Teaching jobs, like all jobs, were in short supply. There had been a scramble for positions advertised earlier in the year; now that the school year was actually underway, those who had failed to get places had given up hope and were desperate for employment—desperate enough to consider our isolated way of life and the salary offered. For as my mother pointed out, eighty dollars a month wasn't really a lot of money. So she advertised, chose a perfectly satisfactory candidate (who much later became a professor at Columbia University in New York!) and by October we children had all been introduced to formal education. Since none of us aspired to be neurosurgeons, and since there was no drug problem and no gang warfare, parents and students alike found education to be a very straightforward and stress-free experience. Year after year, our teachers were young, lively and resourceful. They taught seven or eight children, in five or six grades, the basics and whatever extra their talents could provide. If our grasp of history was a bit tenuous, our knowledge of frog spawn was complete. We missed a lot. We weren't exposed to great music or introduced to the wonders of a library, but we found these things later for ourselves; in the meantime, we learned to work on our own, to think for ourselves and to help the younger members of the class. Except for the time a teacher slipped on a patch of ice, fell on me and broke my collarbone, my education proceeded without incident.

In school or out of it, physical activities didn't include organized sports. Sports, as such, were as foreign to us as a night at the opera, for several reasons. We were all of elementary school age; there were often no teenagers in the community to introduce us to

such things as baseball. Those teenagers who occasionally lived among us did hard physical work all week, and in their few hours of leisure they were more inclined to lie down and read pulp magazines or do their laundry. Then, even if there were an enthusiast or two among the adults, there was no suitable space. Our playing field was not only not level, it was vertical. And finally, and perhaps most importantly, we children had so many more interesting things to do that organized games palled by comparison. No book of children's adventure stories offered experiences that we couldn't duplicate for ourselves. We built log cabins, explored the trackless jungle, dammed streams and played Robinson Crusoe on deserted beaches.

The ocean was too cold for swimming; instead it offered another recreational opportunity. Under the dock, down in the clear green depths, a dazzling array of marine life presented itself—sea urchins, crabs, sea anenomes, starfish, barnacles (which made excellent bait) and rock cod. The fishermen among us bought fishing line from the store, keeping it, when not in use, wound around a bit of scrap lumber. Thus equipped, they spent hours fishing through the cracks in the dock and were invariably rewarded for their patience.

Even the youngest of us pursued their interests with enthusiasm. One little boy of about three, whom my father had nicknamed "Hardtack" for his tough and independent spirit, roamed the bushes and the boardwalk with very little supervision. His abiding interest was natural history, and at regular intervals, tottering the considerable distance between his house and ours, he would proceed to a stump in our front garden. Between the roots, at the base of the stump, was a small opening. "Hardtack" would lie on the ground, head turned and pressed against the stump, and would insert his small arm into this crack and probe about earnestly. Sometimes he would withdraw his arm and try to peer into the blackness within, only to resume his efforts, his arm stretched to its limit.

My mother, seeing his tow head at the back door, knew just what to expect—and she would cringe. Hardtack would hammer on the door with his free hand, and when my mother appeared he would extend the other with its writhing prize.

"Nake,.....nake," he would say, proudly.

"Yes, Hardtack," my mother would say, backing into the laundry tubs, "a very lovely snake. Now put it back where you found it."

Hardtack always did as he was told, but in a week

Under the dock a dazzling array of marine life presented itself. The fishermen among us were invariably rewarded for their patience.

or so the whole process was repeated. The snake's refusal to abandon its chosen home in the face of these disruptions can be interpreted as heroism, or obstinacy—or as proof that reptiles have limited reasoning power.

While most city children have only a hazy idea of what their fathers do all day—and in the 1990s often their mothers as well— we children were anything but vague about our parents' occupations. On one side of the harbour stood the mill, on the other side the mill office and the dock. Everyone's father left the house when the 7:50 mill whistle blew and tramped along the boardwalk to one or other of these destinations. If there was any doubt about what employed them for the rest of the day we could check it out and, in fact, we regularly did.

Everybody's work, with the exception of the bookkeeper's and the storekeeper's, involved noise and machinery; it was heavy and dangerous; it was fun to watch. In the mill, the most interesting person to watch was the sawyer. He stood behind a screen in a welter of noise and a stinging fan of flying sawdust. Just ahead of him whirled two five-foot circular head-saws. The fact that every sawyer was missing fingers proved the unforgiving nature of those saws. Beside the sawyer, and at his bidding, the carriage strained forward carrying a log through the saws, and then raced backwards. Standing on the carriage, balanced and braced against its movement, the dogger made

instant adjustments in response to the sawyer's hand signals. It was a spell-binding ballet.

At the other side of the harbour, the tug wrestled log booms in through the narrow entrance and scows out of it. Like a sheepdog, she circled the perimeter of her charges, pushing here and shoving there. Periodically, she put on an even more entertaining show when our wooden scows had to be turned over for their annual tarring. They were first filled with sea-water, then out in the entrance of the bay the tug put a short tow-line on the half-sunken craft and revved up her engine. The whole scow lifted slowly out of the water like a great black whale and rolled over. Once the bottom was re-tarred, there was a repeat performance to get the scow upright again.

When the tug wasn't towing she was being loaded with lumber. At high tide she lay almost level with the dock, but at low tide she lay a good fifteen feet below it and the slingloads of stacked lumber swung out high in the air before they were lowered to their resting place on the stern deck. If the slings were placed dead centre on the stack of lumber and the load was thus perfectly balanced, it was easy enough to handle; but an unbalanced load, once lifted off the ground, acted like an unbroken horse, willfully catching on every protuberance, dragging its hapless attendant hither and yon. Once over the edge of the dock, it took up a vertical position rather than a horizontal one, and threatened to slide downward onto the heads of those below. Again men and machines performed their intricate dance: the tug's engine puffed away in neutral, the winch growled, the boom swung back and forth, hands signalled, feet kept carefully out of the bight of the line.

All day long there was the reassuring hum of machinery with the clack of conveyors and the whining of saws providing grace notes. As a child, I was always disturbed by communities where earning a living wasn't accompanied by noise. I found their atmosphere purposeless and their silence depressing.

People never believe me when I say I can't ride a bicycle.

"What do you mean?" they say irritably. "Everyone can ride a bicycle. I've been riding a bicycle since I was six."

Well, I haven't. I can't ride a bicycle because where I grew up there were no roads. None. That's the message my mother finally got across to the Superintendent of Education. There was an icy ocean sloshing at the rocks and a dense wall of cedar, fir, hemlock and salal right down to the high-water mark. There were floats and gangways and docks and a boardwalk that was supported by pilings, but there was no road. No possible way to leave the confines of that small horseshoe-shaped cove, except by water.

Bea and I didn't have bicycles; instead we had a flat-bottomed twelve-foot skiff. It was old and heavy and so badly designed that it was like rowing an island, but it gave us freedom and a clumsy mobility. Not that there weren't ground rules. We were taught never to stand up in a rowboat, never to run on a larger boat, never to play on log booms (logs having a tendency to roll you off into the water and then close over your head), and never, *ever* to scream. We kept our shrill children's voices down. We knew that it we ever needed help that would be the time to scream. Our home was always filled with my parents' friends, and when these were city people,

their children, hummed up by the novelty of it all, ran up and down the deck of the tug screeching endlessly. We regarded them gravely, and with a certain amount of contempt.

Day after day, weather permitting, my sister and I sallied forth in our skiff. There was no real destination possible, for the coastline was deserted on both sides of our harbour. Instead of going somewhere, we examined starfish and at low tide knocked abalone off the bottom with one swift jab of an oar. We made kelp babies from the huge globes of kelp with their briny streaming hair, we watched whales before it was fashionable to do so, and we kept an eye on the tide.

The tide ruled out lives. Those unfamiliar with BC coastal water were always astounded by their tidal currents. Not for nothing were our docks built to accommodate a twenty-two foot rise and fall. From a distance, the ocean appeared static and for a few minutes twice a day it was; but the innocents who found themselves out in a rowboat when the tide turned and started to run had the unsettling experience of rowing as hard as they could in one direction while being swept inexorably in the opposite one, and were the source of much amusement until they learned better. Small whirlpools, forming and reforming around the boat, were nature's reminder that this was one big river that wouldn't alter its direction for another twelve hours.

Of course, an engine would have changed all this, but in the 1930's outboards were rare and notoriously

My sister, myself, our rowboat and the makings of a kelp doll.

unreliable. More important, they were expensive; during the Depression there was no money for recreation—or even for conveniences. Hard labour was the substitute. And so my sister and I considered ourselves very fortunate in having the luxury of our own boat. We rowed for miles and, of necessity, we watched the tides. We knew when they were slack, when they would be working to our advantage and how, if all else failed, we could get in very close to shore and pick up a back eddy. None of this was taught, but was simply learned from watching a parent who did not row, but who ran a tug and made part of his living towing booms of logs and scows.

On one of our expeditions we took our dog, Puppy, with us. He was anything but a puppy. Our previous dogs, Yissie and Cultus, had been killed by cougars. Puppy was, as my grandmother termed it, a Jap dog. He had belonged to a departed Japanese fam-

Alex MacDonald and I in the millyard with Yissie and Cultus, Both dogs were later killed by cougars.

ily—hence his generic name, I suppose—who had left him behind. He was a very solid dog—the word stout comes to mind—and an ocean voyage was a pleasant novelty for him. He sat in the bow seat of our stubby little boat and regarded the watery world with interest. Suddenly, directly in front of him, not three feet away, a large salmon jumped into the air and hit the water with a splash. Puppy let out a series of wild barks and leaped over the bow in the general direction of the salmon. When he surfaced, he was paddling hard—and grunting, the frigid water and his new form of locomotion causing him acute anxiety. He had completely forgotten the salmon and wanted just one thing, to get back into the skiff. Realizing that we would capsize if we tried to pull him over the side, we spun the boat around and approached him stern first. Country dogs don't wear collars, so there was nothing to grasp. The one who was not at the oars leaned over, grabbed him by the leg and pulled. Feeling in imminent danger of having his leg yanked out of its socket, Puppy wisely resisted. Maybe a rope, we thought; all we had was our painter. The oarsman reversed the skiff and now approached Puppy bow on. The rope approach was as futile as the leg approach. There was no way we could reach far enough to secure the painter around Puppy's ample middle. All three of us were becoming exceedingly anxious. Once more we spun the boat around and approached Puppy stern to. Now we both crouched in the stern seat, balancing our weight as evenly as possible. Without a word, we both reached out our skinny arms, grabbed Puppy by the rolls of fat around his non-existent neck and hauled with a strength born of desperation. Puppy came scrabbling into the boat, clawing us painfully in the process and streaming cold water. For the rest of the voyage, we took turns rowing and sitting in the stern seat with our arms held firmly around Puppy's wet neck. Although he seemed disinclined to repeat the performance, we were taking no chances.

All of our efforts, that day and on other similar jaunts, were hampered by the fact that Bea and I were wearing bulky homemade life-jackets. There were no child-sized life-jackets in the 1930s. For economic reasons, recreational boating wasn't a feature of those years, and children who lived as my sister and I did represented an infinitesimal share of the life-jacket market. So my mother, ever resourceful, bought some heavy white canvas and sewed it into child-sized vests. She ripped open one or two of the older, grubbier vests that we carried on the *Klinekwa* and inserted slabs of cork, sewing them firmly into place. We wore them for two reasons. Firstly we knew the dangers the sea presented. The local doctor calculated that anyone thrown into it had twenty minutes of life before dying of hypothermia. The comments of city-dwelling relatives of local drowning victims, that they "couldn't understand how this could happen. He was a very strong swimmer," made no sense to us. We could understand all too well how such things could happen, and we understood, too, that our life-jackets were no guarantee of survival. They simply gave us an edge of safety.

The second reason we wore our life-jackets was that our mother wouldn't have let us out on the water without them. That she let us go alone, at all, is a source of wonderment to me now, for she was a conscientious and protective parent, inordinately concerned with germs and other lurking dangers. However, given the circumstances of our life, I suppose she saw nothing unusual about two skinny little girls in a twelve-foot rowboat exploring miles of coastline, out of the sight or hearing of all other human beings.

As we got older, our expeditions took on a much more business-like air, for our father now offered us real money for any beachcomb logs we brought in. By this time our heavy little skiff had been replaced by a big old open boat with a little two-hp Briggs & Stratton engine. Emboldened by the knowledge that we now had power and were not at the mercy of the tides, and dazzled by the prospect of being paid the going price for logs and of earning the astounding sum of ninety dollars for a big one, we pursued this new avocation with enthusiasm. There were only two provisos: from mother, the usual admonition about wearing our life-jackets; from father, a stern warning that we were not to use our oars—which we always carried for back-up should the Briggs & Stratton fail—to pry logs off the beach.

Each afternoon after school we would race home, change our clothes and putt-putt out of the cove, around the point and into the open strait in search of "a good log." Our voyages were not without incident.

One sunny afternoon we spotted a gigantic fir log drifting lazily down the strait. We cut the engine and maneuvered alongside it. Even rough calculations promised hundreds of board feet of prime fir. We got our tow rope around it, fastened it securely with a timber hitch and then moved to start the engine. The starting cord had to be wrapped around the flywheel

and then yanked briskly. Sometimes one yank would do it, but if the plugs were dirty it might take several to get it to spring into action. This time the first yank failed and, as the flywheel reversed itself, it whipped the starting cord through the air and wedged its small wooden handle beneath the floorboards of the boat. One would assume that if the handle had gotten in under the floorboards it could be gotten out. Not easily, we discovered. The flywheel's force had driven it far into a crack and it was severely stuck. This, in itself, posed no particular problem; the urgency lay in the fact that, as we wrestled with the engine, the tide turned. Slowly, but with increasing velocity, it moved our little boat and its huge tow around and around down the strait. As we struggled with the jammed cord, small whirlpools appeared around us and the distant shoreline moved past in the wrong direction. By the time the handle was finally extricated and the engine started, we were a couple of miles from our starting point. Gradually we took up the slack on our tow rope and gave the engine its maximum two horsepower. Slowly, at full throttle, we slipped backwards down the strait. Our little engine could buck the tide unencumbered, but towing a giant log rendered it impotent. We had drifted so far from home that we were now concerned about our gas supply. There was only one thing to do. With keen regret we cut the engine once again, untied the log, re-started the engine, being careful to cover the floorboards with a jacket to prevent further mishap, and headed for home. We were bucking a strong tide now and our progress was slow. Behind us, our three hundred dollar log, the source of unimaginable wealth, the basis of our future fortune, whirled lazily round and round in the current until we could no longer see it at all.

We had other beachcombing problems. One afternoon, attempting to roll a log off the rocky shoreline and into the water, the temptation to use the oar as a pry grew too strong; I did what I'd been told not to do with predictable results. The oar broke and the log stayed right where it was. I was disturbed but determined. I searched the shoreline for a piece of driftwood that would serve as a pry and renewed my efforts to free the log. Then one of my feet slipped on the kelp that covered the rocks and, looking down, I saw that my leg had taken on a peculiar configuration. I suspected I had dislocated my knee. It was extremely painful but I dared not cry or even appear unduly upset. Bea, five years younger that I, was the only source of help, and I was afraid that if I alarmed her she might not act with the dispatch and efficiency required. I got myself firmly seated on a log and, trying hard for nonchalance, I said, "Bea, I think I've hurt my knee. Will you pick up my foot and pull it out, towards you, just as hard as you can? Pull it really hard," I said, anxiously. She did just that and with the resilience of all things youthful it snapped back into position. Now she put the pieces of the broken oar into the boat and I eased myself down the rocks and over the gunwale. We started the engine and headed home in a very subdued mood. I knew my father would be extremely annoyed about the oar, my knee was throbbing painfully, and our log remained where we had found it, securely wedged in the rocks.

As we approached our teen years, Bea and I learned to swim in a public pool in Victoria. This was considered not so much a recreational experience, but rather, a means of ensuring our survival. As our proficiency in the water improved my mother relaxed her insistence on life-jackets. First, as the oldest, I was permitted to go without mine, which made it all the more onerous for my sister to have to wear hers. One day when we were on some family trip on the tug, my sister prevailed upon mother to let her out of this constriction.

"Well, yes," said mother, "I guess you're old enough to be on the boat without your life-jacket..." Jubilant, my sister ripped off the offending garment and flung it overboard. We watched with shock and fascination as it sank like a stone beneath the wake of the tug.

IV

THE SIMPLE LIFE

Weynton Passage—This passage leads northwestward from the junction of Johnstone Strait and Broughton Strait into Blackfish Sound and the eastern end of Cormorant Channel. The fairway, which is deep, has a minimum width of 7 cables. In Weynton Passage, the tidal streams attain a velocity of 5 knots at times, and set over and across the shoals extending from Stephenson Islet. There are heavy tide rips at times near both shores, and in the vicinity of Stubbs Island.

British Columbia Pilot

Searching records of the past brings the bewildering feeling that Telegraph Cove never existed, that these men and women and children never lived. In libraries there are one or two newspaper articles written long after the fact. In the provincial Archives, there are my grandfather's notes to his friend Major J.S. Matthews. There is a sentence or two in the *British Columbia Pilot*. And that is all. It's as if the whole thing were a figment of the imagination; and yet, day and night, with a billow of smoke or a shower of sparks, the sawmill burner advertised our presence. By day, we were a cluster of small brown buildings and a dock huddled at the base of a mountain. By night, we were a few dim lights in the miles and miles of blackness.

Every day of the week but one, men hefted timbers in the rain and wrestled with second-hand machinery. Their wives tried to get one Monday's wash dry before the next Monday rolled around, and had their babies as cheaply as possible—one inadvertently giving birth in the sawdust of the mill floor. After school, we children helped at home and engaged in our own strenuous projects. One January, for example, we formed a bucket brigade and emptied the frog pond onto the ground in a misguided attempt to create a skating rink.

Our hard work was our security. We produced something tangible and were paid for it. We each had a house to call our own and a kitchen stove to fill the rooms with warmth and drive away the dampness. These basics were our bulwark against the times, for in the cities people were lining up at soup kitchens, and on the prairies some of them were starving.

Although our little community had intruded to

some small degree, the landscape belonged to the natural world and its inhabitants. Raccoons boldly picked our raspberries in full view of their rightful owners, deer demolished our roses, otters played on our log booms and cougars prowled our woods and occasionally ate our pets. If they were hungry enough, they tried to eat people as well, as Hillier Lansdowne discovered. "Hilly" was a descendant of the illustrious and aristocratic British Lansdownes, although the connection was not immediately apparent when you met him. He had a small logging camp on one of the islands across the strait, where one morning a cougar leapt out of the woods and attacked Mrs. Coon, the wife of one of the Indian loggers. Although he had no gun or any other weapon at hand, Hilly rushed to her rescue. By this time the cougar's jaws had a firm grip on the woman's shoulder. Hilly got his hands around both sides of the animal's neck and, after some considerable effort, strangled it. He brushed off any suggestion of exceptional bravery. "Since I outweighed the son-of-a-bitch by about a hundred pounds, I expected to win that fight," was his comment.

Visitors found all of this madly picturesque. People tend to romanticize what they don't understand, and they certainly didn't understand our life. They walked into our shabby kitchen, smelled bread baking and were enchanted. "Back to the simple life," they enthused. But it wasn't a simple life; it was actually very complicated, and it stretched our capabilities to the limit. Or our guests gazed out at the view from our living-room windows and said, "It's just breathtakingly beautiful, of course, but what do you do to fill your time?" Somehow it escaped their notice that at that very moment my mother was filling her time by doing what she did so often—cooking dinner for a crowd. And perhaps cooking it on a sawdust burning stove that wasn't burning because the sawdust was wet hemlock. Her culinary tasks were always made especially difficult when the sawmill was cutting hemlock.

My mother's chief source of dissatisfaction however, was not the saw-dust burner, but the house itself. It was far too small and very ugly, for it was still essentially a lineman's shack. My mother's grandfather had been an architect and she had inherited his eye. She spent all her spare moments drawing floor plans, clipping pictures and planning her dream home. At first she thought that a log house would be the most suited to our environment, but my father said that log construction was poor advertising for a sawmill, so then she dreamed of a Dutch Colonial. She got neither. It was ironic that someone who cared so much about houses should live all her married life in one of the ugliest buildings imaginable.

It must have been about 1932 that my father and Alex MacDonald went to look at the boilers at Suquash, and there my mother and I found a real-life dream home. I can date it because I can remember it so I must have been about three.

The men had heard that the abandoned coal mine there was selling two brand new boilers at a bargain price, so a "picnic" was organized one weekend and we took the boat to Suquash, anchored and rowed in to shore. While the men went off to inspect the boilers, my mother and I investigated the big house that sat empty on a rise above the sea. Much later. when I explored the interior of BC, where there are so many more mines, I was always puzzled by the difference in the quality of the housing provided for the managers of mines compared to what was laid on for those who managed logging operations—and I'm still puzzled. Whereas the superintendent of even a large logging camp lived in a tacky little frame house, the manager of any mine lived in a house that verged on the luxurious. The house we found at Suquash was a perfect example. We pushed open the door and went inside and, even as a small child, I knew that this was what was left of a lovely home. The walls were panelled, there were square bay windows with window seats, and a huge river rock fireplace capable of supplying endless cheer in the unendingly rainy climate. Indians had been in the house before us and had ripped off some of the panelling for firewood. They had cooked clams in the great fireplace, and the shells were piled high on the hearth. I loved the house and couldn't understand why it had been abandoned by its occupants. For Emma, living in her ugly shack, it must have been an even more painful experience to wander through those empty rooms. However, she said nothing; she simply took a photo of the great stone fireplace and we turned and left the house to its fate.

Finally, in 1937, my father came up with what he considered a brilliant solution to the housing problem. He would have Mame's brother, who was also named Fred, raise our house and put another storey under it. As a consequence what started out as a lineman's shack ended up as a large two-

The added storey at least made the lineman's shack into more of a family home.

storey lineman's shack.

The whole undertaking was an ambitious one and certainly wouldn't have been possible without the skill of my father's uncle. This remarkable man, with nothing more than a couple of pump jacks and a big pile of mill ends, cut the house loose from its moorings and raised it eight feet into the air. The fact that it stood on an irregularly shaped rock bluff (as rock bluffs usually are) didn't make the job any easier.

While all this was going on, my father lived in the upper part of the building. Having the rest of us do the same thing must have seemed, even to him, to be stretching the point a bit, so my mother, my sister and I spent the summer in Victoria. My father kept us posted. He wrote to my mother:

Was glad to get your letter today and if we had four or five carpenters here might be able to keep up with your suggestions but we are following as closely as we can and doing our very best. Some of the minor ideas we can leave for awhile but just for now Fred is getting in the plumbing which I miss terribly. The house looks funny now from the outside—like a box but when Fred gets those false eaves on I think it will be fine. Our old bedroom is as good as new, just has to be nailed on to the house again. (It had been removed from the now-second storey in order to maintain a rectangle and was now going to be re-attached to the ground floor!)

To me he wrote:

You would have a great time if you were here now. Every time you wanted to go in the house you would have to climb up the woodshed roof and in our bedroom window. The King and Queen are looking out over the roof and you have to crawl into that room from the basement. Some morning I expect to wake up and find I can't get out at all. The black cat doesn't know what to make of it all.

We returned to a house with five bedrooms, two bathrooms, some very nice French doors leading from the front hall to the living-room and a fireplace. It wasn't, however, by any stretch of the imagination, a Dutch Colonial.

By now our little ten-hp Petters light engine had been replaced with a new larger one. The "new" light engine was, of course, not new but was the Atlas Imperial that had formerly powered the *Sundown;* nor did it give us much more access to the wonders of electricity. The community was allowed electricity for one morning a week for

The mine manager's house at Suquash. The stair railings and panelling had been used for firewood and the hearth was littered with clamshells.

domestic purposes and, as a consequence, half a dozen frantic housewives plugged in their washing machines at the same time, which often proved more than the generator could bear and left us with a tub full of washing and no power.

For this reason, electricity played a very small part in our housekeeping. We kept our perishables in a screened safe, ironed our clothes with sad irons, cooked on a sawdust burner and took our rugs outdoors to beat them free of dust. When the incessant rain made clothes drying outdoors impossible, we hung the laundry on a ceiling rack in the kitchen and dodged wet sheets as we cooked. In place of a vacuum cleaner, we filled a bucket with damp shreds of torn newspapers, scattered these over the fir floors and then swept them up along with the dust that clung to them. At an early age I was practised in all these domestic arts, and I could run a winch and load a boat with lumber as well, but when I went to high school in Victoria, I found these to be non-transferable skills.

Given this casual country life and the absence of labour-saving appliances, the housewife of today would adopt a casual country style and use pottery and table mats. No one had this imagination or good sense in the 1930s; instead, we used white damask tablecloths and napkins, silver flatware and, for Sunday dinner, white and gold Limoges china. It made for a lot of unnecessary work. Nor did we use any better sense when it came to food.

If we on the north Island were poor in monetary terms, we were immensely rich when it came to natural resources. Year after year, seiners dotted the waters of Johnstone Strait and hauled in nets full of salmon; in Belize Inlet, prawn fishermen caught eighteen hundred pounds of prawns in four days; the local paper bragged that our timber resources could "build a boardwalk to the moon." Our tiny population took all this largesse for granted and saw no end to its abundance. Yet, as a family, we certainly didn't take advantage of it. Far from living off the land, we ate cases of canned vegetables and a lot of gristly roast beef, and if we had had to depend on my father to catch us a fish or shoot us a deer we would have long since starved. The only people who really understood how to live off these resources were our Japanese employees.

At eleven o'clock each evening, our electric lights faded once as a warning and then went out. What had been a cheerily lit living-room moments before was plunged into the deep darkness of a country night until, with much stumbling and fumbling, the coal oil lamps were lit. Guests from the city found this delightfully idiosyncratic—so amusing and romantic to carry a lamp upstairs to bed. This return to the lamplight of yesteryear wasn't, as one might guess, an effort to save on the fuel that powered the light engine; rather it was insurance against our being burned in our beds. Our house, and all the other buildings in the community, had been wired by amateurs. Even someone of my father's optimistic nature felt that the sleeping occupants were safer without power surging through this creative electrical work.

We were lucky at Telegraph Cove in that, before roads and radio-telephones and helicopters, we had two life-lines that many coastal communities did not. We had a sixty-foot boat that was well maintained and operated by someone with skill and judgement—and we had a telephone. The telephone line was simply strung along the coastline, and was frequently taken out by falling trees. Each party was assigned a particular series of rings—we answered our phone when it rang one short and one long ring—and to call others we cranked out the appropriate rings. Everyone on the line could listen to everyone else if they were so inclined—but they weren't, probably because the phone was never used for casual conversation. It was for business or for emergencies, and it surprised no one when it was dead and couldn't be used at all until the lineman, patrolling by boat, found the break and fixed it.

Then, in the early 1940s, Spilsbury and Hepburn began to install a magical new device called a radio-telephone in all the isolated habitations that dotted the coast. Up until that time, people in the remote settlements were cut off from the rest of the world by distance and silence. Suddenly that silence was broken, communication was possible, distance shrank. Life would never again be quite so sternly lonely. The radio-phones facilitated business, of course, but for people engaged in work as dangerous as logging, people whose only previous connection with civilization was a gasboat, they could also mean the difference between life and death.

Since we were connected to the telephone line we continued to use that form of communication, but we had a radio-telephone installed in the boat, as did almost everyone else. Now, when we were off on our various trips, we could listen to the marine weather reports and notify customers of our estimated time of arrival. And we could relieve the tedium of towing by listening to fishing boats, separated by a distance of two miles, enquiring, with unconcealed delight at this new toy, "How's the weather over there?" Although this was a straightforward (though superfluous) question, there was a lot of duplicity wafting over the radio waves, too. Passing a seiner brailing in enough salmon to sink it, we could hear her skipper being evasive about his position and success, in order to keep his fellows as far away as possible.

Listening in, of course, was quite acceptable,

because to make a call one had to wait until any existing conversation was completed. And only half of the conversation was actually heard. The other half was merely a series of beeps and had to be imagined. That this was not a real limitation was exemplified by a conversation we overheard one day between a man on a fish packer and his wife in Vancouver. We could hear only the wife's side of the conversation.

She said she missed him.

A couple of perfunctory beeps.

She found herself greatly inconvenienced in his long absences by her inability to drive a car.

Three beeps.

She would like to learn to drive.

Three beeps.

The man next door had offered to teach her. How did this idea strike him?

A torrent of beeps poured from the marine band.....

Our other connections with the larger world were the daily newspaper and the radio, but neither one came to us as straightforwardly as city-dwellers were used to. The newspapers arrived once a week on a Union steamship, in a big bundle containing the previous seven days' news. This was not an unsatisfactory arrangement. There is something infinitely relaxing about reading news that's a week old. As if we weren't distanced enough from the alarums of the world, this distanced us even more. There was rarely a problem that hadn't been resolved by the time we read about it. My grandfather, in particular, sitting in front of the fire, puffing his pipe and reading the week-old newspapers, found the time lapse just right for his stage of life.

The radio, a floor model Stromberg Carlson, had two limitations. Firstly, it was powered by a storage battery which gave us a week or two of strong reception and then, as the battery weakened, just a few tantalizing moments of sound before it faded away to nothing; and secondly, since we lived right at the base of a mountain, radio reception was uniformly poor and no amount of amateur aerial adjusting could overcome the challenge of topography.

Our contact with the outside world via the media, then, was sporadic, limited, out-of-date and filled with static. Our contact with the rest of the human race, however, was continuous and immediate. Each visitor who appeared at our door had come a long way to get there; the wonder of it was that there were so many of them. Without warning, pile-driver operators, yachtsmen, school teachers, wire rope salesmen and clergymen, to name a few, turned up on our doorstep. As a consequence, growing up in our house was a lot like working in a hotel. If our visitors were stranded, they were offered a bed; if they were cruising in a small boat they were offered a bath; all of them were offered a meal. We had a visitor, or visitors, for at least one meal a day—sometimes for all three. Because we owned the store, we had access to groceries twenty-four hours a day. That was a good thing, because in the kitchen a meal planned for five became one for eight; the breakfast porridge for four was stretched, with piles of toast, to feed six; extra pies, cakes and cookies rolled out of the oven, and the dirty dishes formed an endless stream. All of this was accomplished with a sawdust-burning cookstove, a far from inexhaustible supply of hot water provided by that same stove, and no electrical appliances.

Having this throng of dissimilar people passing through the house meant that we learned, like Barbara Walters, to make conversation with anyone about anything. And it meant that, to this day, I have a compulsion to ask anyone who appears at the door to come in for a meal.

Mother had been raised a Methodist, but she switched to the Anglican church when she married. I was glad she did, because Methodists were very strict and forbade card playing and dancing, which seemed to me to put quite a damper on a life that wasn't already over-filled with entertainment. Besides, the Church of England appeared to be the official religion of the north coast. This was because their missionaries had got there first. In Alert Bay, they had built an Indian residential school, a much-needed hospital and a small but beautiful church. And then, in the early years at least, they sent the clergy for this church directly out from England.

Unlike their brethren who joined the army and set out for India, these men hadn't joined the church for adventure, so the difference between life in a quiet English village and life on the BC coast left them in a permanent state of culture shock. It made them an easy target for ridicule, too, which didn't help the religion they were promoting. Like our table linen, they were nice but unsuited to the surroundings.

They were also hard to talk to. They were the only visitors who defeated our Barbara Walters-ish attempts at conversation. Sitting in our living-room, sipping tea and eating cucumber sandwiches (which my mother thought would make them feel at home) we had absolutely nothing to say to each other. After a couple of hours of this, we felt we had done our bit for the Anglican church.

We had better luck with the mission boat *Columbia* which brought us the Rev. Heber Greene, who was equally sincere but much more suited to the environment. Still, it isn't any of his religious teachings that I remember. Rather, I remember watching in awe as Rev. Greene, sitting at our breakfast table, put cream and brown sugar on his bowl of oatmeal and then poured his glass of orange juice over it. "It will all end up in the same place," he said cheerfully.

A scow load of lumber and a scow load of slabs, mid-'30s. The latter were sold to the Indian Residential School at Alert Bay to fuel their heating plant.

V

MARINE TRAFFIC

Johnstone Strait—The southern shore is a continuous series of high, steep mountain ranges rising abruptly from the water's edge, some of the highest peaks being covered with snow all year round. These ranges are separated by valleys through which flow streams of considerable size.

British Columbia Pilot

All along the northeast coast of Vancouver Island, the mountains drop straight into the sea. At the foot of one of them, our small horseshoe-shaped harbour looked out, due north, onto Johnstone Strait. It was a stunning view. Beyond the strait lay the delicate outline of an intricate web of islands; beyond that lay the mainland and the coast mountains. Mount Waddington, the highest peak in the range rose, like Mount Fuji, in the distance.

Johnstone Strait was our thoroughfare, our link with the rest of humanity. In theory, it could have started us on a journey to the ends of the earth, and in practice it sometimes brought us ships from just such places. We travelled Johnstone Strait to shop, to do business, to visit friends, to see a doctor, or just to while away a Sunday afternoon. On sunny summer mornings when the sea was glassy and rolled away from a boat's bow in oily curves, on bright fall afternoons when the westerlies got up as regularly as clockwork and blew the sea into a blazing blue, or on bleak November days when the southeasters shook the house and turned the sea into an army of great grey rollers smoking with spume; at all these times, in a variety of craft, we emerged into the strait on our errands, be they casual or critical.

A constant stream of marine traffic worked its way up and down the strait: freighters, passenger steamers, tugs and tows, seiners, trollers and yachts. Some of these vessels called in at our little harbour at regular intervals, some simply passed by, and some of them appeared unexpectedly from nowhere, moored for an hour, a week or a summer, and then vanished as completely as if they had never existed.

The most regular of our callers were the Union steamships. Each week, without fail, either the *Cardena* or the *Catala* arrived. Their black hulls, white superstructures and red funnels were familiar to every coastal inhabitant, for they were the north coast's supply line to the city. Each week on "boat day," the ship's radio operator broadcast the estimated time of arrival and then, there they were, rounding the point and blocking the entrance to the harbour with their bulk. Suddenly the air was full of acrid smoke from their funnels, the store was full of fresh food, and the Post Office was full of the mail they delivered.

As children, we made many trips with our mother to and from Vancouver on these ships, and they were always thrilling adventures. Encumbered as we often were by an aged aunt—and sometimes even a canary—we required two staterooms. My sister and I shared one of them, revelling in our independence. However, when it came time to go to bed, we needed help from an adult. Employing some secret procedure that died with them, the stewards on these ships made up the berths so tightly that it took a strong and determined adult to pry the sheets apart. No child was equal to the task. Even when one finally wriggled in under the blankets, it was only those with the general body contours of a postage stamp who could be comfortable.

We were shy country children, and when we descended the broad brass-trimmed stairway to the dining saloon we were always overwhelmed by its magnificence. There were big, round tables with snowy napery, clusters of silver cutlery, glasses tinkling with ice cubes, and stewards in black uniforms and immaculate white shirts. The menu always included the item "celery and olives" and we astonished our adult table-mates by quietly devouring every olive in sight. Travelling thus we had acquired a taste for them and we never, ever, had them at home.

In retrospect, the service that the Union Steamship Company provided was remarkable. They pressed doggedly on through violent winter storms and, perhaps even more remarkably, they kept to their appointed schedules in blankets of fog. Long before radar, these sizeable ships negotiated the convoluted channels and narrow passages that formed our difficult coast, and made their regular appearances in the tiniest, most remote settlement. Year after year, with no fanfare and little recognition, their tired-looking captains performed remarkable feats of seamanship.

The company didn't operate entirely without incident, of course. Although we ourselves had never been involved in any of their marine mishaps, an acquaintance of ours had.

Mr. Pesnic was a huge, raw-boned man in his seventies who had been a logger and a homesteader. He had a booming voice, a thick middle-European accent, and a unique pattern of stress and intonation that made his conversation particularly compelling and invariably reduced my father to helpless laughter,

no matter how mundane the subject. Sitting chatting on his back steps one day he happened to mention that he had been on the Union steamship *Cheslakee* when she sank at the dock at Van Anda. My father sensed that a man of Pesnic's phlegmatic temperament might possibly provide an uncommon perspective on the event and he was absolutely right.

Mr. Pesnic, it appeared, had left Vancouver on the 8:45 p.m. sailing. He went to bed in his cabin, planning to get off at Manson's Landing on Cortes Island early the next morning. Once into Georgia Strait, the *Cheslakee* encountered grimly heavy weather. Hit by one particularly bad squall, her cargo shifted and she couldn't be righted. Asleep in his bunk, Mr. Pesnic was unaware of these grave events, but when he finally awoke it was to a feeling of unease. The ship was docked, but not at Manson's Landing. A great deal of shouting and commotion was going on outside the porthole, and the floor of his cabin was not in the same position as it had been the night before. With some difficulty, Pesnic got out of his berth, put on some clothes, struggled out into the corridor, up the companionway and onto the deck. A scene of considerable chaos met his eyes. The ship was heeling over, and as the deck slanted ever more

The Union steamship S.S. *Cheslakee* when she sank at the dock at Van Anda, January 1913.

markedly, passengers were clambering up it in a desperate attempt to reach the ladder on the dock.

Obviously, the women passengers were having the most difficult time. Pesnic had probably never heard the expression "women and children first," but he subscribed to the idea. He and another man helped the women to get themselves and their families up the deck and onto the ladder. Nor did they confine their efforts to women. A man in city clothes, who seemed to be reacting quite emotionally to the whole experience, was also helped to the ladder. He climbed to the top, walked across the dock in a state of shock and fell into the water on the other side. There he clung to a piling screaming for help.

"Shut up!" bellowed Pesnic. "We saved you once. You're just going to have to wait."

By now the deck had assumed an almost perpendicular position, and Pesnic decided that the time had come to save himself. He got a firm grip on a hatch cover that was now above his head rather than in its customary position underfoot, and tried to haul himself up. Some distance above him was a logger with the same intent. When that logger had thrown on his clothes that morning they included the only footwear that he had—a pair of heavy caulk boots with razor sharp nails protruding from the soles. They give the wearer a firm grip on a log but they don't give much purchase on a steel deck. Besides, the logger was inclining just a bit towards panic. He scrabbled up the deck, slipped and came crashing down on Pesnic's fingers.

"*Well* now," Pesnic explained to my father, "he was a big man and I got sort of mad."

Once again the man scrambled for safety, and once again he fell back onto Pesnic's fingers.

"You bastard," shouted Pesnic, finally provoked, "you wait till I get up there! I will give you a punch you won't forget."

"What happened?" asked my father, who was at this point convulsed with laughter.

"When I finally got up on that dock," said Pesnic, "the bugger was gone."

My father composed himself, we had a cup of Mr. Pesnic's good strong coffee and walked back to our boat.

Unlike the Union steamships, most of the boats that called came unexpectedly. Waking to a strong southeaster, we might find three seiners tied to the dock below the house, their big brailers swaying at their masts, their fishing company flags snapping in the wind. Having sought shelter for the night, they would start up their engines and head out again with daylight. As they let go their lines the incomprehensible shouts of their crews identified them as Italian or Yugoslavian.

When boats arrived at night, they often advertised their presence by flicking on their searchlights and probing the darkness for the narrow entrance to our harbour. Since two of our upstairs bedrooms faced directly out to sea, we would be wakened suddenly from a sound sleep to find the whole room brilliantly illuminated. This blinding light would move back and forth, like a great eye, checking the rocky shore and the docks, and then, having established its boat's position, it would snap off, leaving us to our sleep.

One day a "back to basics" family sailed into the Cove; quite literally, for their vessel had no power, only its sails. Sailboats were a curiosity, since they weren't suitable as workboats and the wealthy, who had money for recreational craft, favoured power boats. The crew of the sailboat consisted of a man, his wife and their son who was about two. They embraced the hippie philosophy of living off the land and they had been subsisting on clams, fish, seaweed and berries—a highly nutritious diet but one that palls after a time. At any rate, they didn't seem averse to joining the market economy, if only temporarily. The husband became one of the sawmill crew and the wife moved—with some relief, it appeared—into one of the employee houses. Here, at least, they had plumbing and more spacious quarters than their boat afforded. It was the child, however, who gained the most from this change of scene. At sea he had played at the nose of the boat, a tiny area fenced off with rope to keep him from falling overboard. He was so used to spending his days sitting down that when he came ashore he continued the practice. It was some time before he recognized the possibilities inherent in standing up and walking around. When they resumed their voyage, which they did before long, it must have been hard for this two-year-old to relinquish his new-found freedom and adjust once more to the boat.

On another day, we woke to find a little boat tied, not to the dock or to the floats, but to a boom-stick on the other side of the bay. For a couple of days there was no sign of life aboard. Finally, worried about its occupant, Jimmy, our boat's engineer, rowed over to investigate. The owner, as small as his little boat, was asleep in his bunk.

"How's your grub?" asked Jimmy, after looking

around the confined space not seeing anything at all that was edible. "Got anything to eat?"

"I've got a bit of flour," said the occupant.

"That doesn't sound like a lot to me," said Jimmy. "You'd better come across and tie your boat to the float and get some food."

And so Tinkerbell, as he was nicknamed, stayed around all summer and did odd jobs. Then, one fall morning, we awoke to find that Tinkerbell, in his little boat with its tiny engine, had sailed away.

Not all our visitors were as impecunious—or as reticent—as Tinkerbell. In summer large, glossy yachts came gliding around the point. Crew members readied snazzy rope bumpers all along their sides, lest anything mar their perfect paintwork; people in bright clothes lounged on their afterdecks. If our boat was out, they sometimes made themselves at home at her mooring. The owner of one of these over-powered toys, having blithely moored in the *Hili-Kum*'s spot, came into the store for ice.

"I'm sorry, we don't have ice," said Thelma, the storekeeper.

"No *ice*?" the man asked, incredulously. He looked around the store as if to assure himself that she wasn't hiding some behind a counter somewhere.

"No ice," said Thelma.

"So, I'll have some gas," the man said. He regarded the store's little display of wilted vegetables with disdain. "You *do* have gas?"

"Yes," said Thelma, "but you'll have to move to the front of the dock."

She got the keys to the gas shed, he moved his boat, and they met at the end of the dock.

"You can fill up the water, too," the man said.

When his gas tank was full, Thelma switched hoses and filled up his water tank. Then they went back to the store where she made out his bill.

"What about the water?" the man said, checking the bill.

"We don't charge for water," said Thelma. "It's just there for our own convenience. We're not really in the tourist business." She was getting her own back.

The word "tourist" did it. The man seemed suddenly compelled to present himself as a master mariner.

"Just came through the Yuculta Rapids," he said, notching up his voice. He pronounced it as it's spelled, which was unfortunate. "We're going to Alaska. Going across the Sound," he added, just in case we yokels thought he was going overland. "Of course, that boat I've got can take anything. I've been out in a lot of dirty weather in that boat."

My father had been working in the office. Now he came around and peered through the Post Office wicket to see where all the noise was coming from.

"Spread it thin," he murmured. "You've got a large farm."

This kind of thing left us members of the "life is real, life is earnest" school with a permanent distaste for high life. Secretly, I took great pride in the fact that ours was a workboat and that, as a consequence, our trips had a purpose. By definition, then, others might be amateurs but we were pros. I never revealed this reverse snobbery to anyone else in the family, and only once do I remember any of them making a comment in this regard. We were tied alongside a big yacht in the some harbour after a very long day on the water and, as my grandmother prepared dinner, she noticed a white uniformed chef doing the same thing in the galley opposite.

"Oh, sometimes I do miss having a Chinaman," she sighed.

Fortunately, there was a different kind of yachtsman we looked forward to seeing and with whom we became fast friends. They were regular visitors—their boats appeared every summer without fail. Most of them were Americans who made the trip up the Inside Passage to Alaska each year. They were competent seamen and interested and interesting people—magazine editors, teachers, professional people of all kinds, who filled our living-room with their adventures, their enthusiasm and their laughter.

Our own boat lay moored at the dock below our house. When the winter southeasters howled up the strait our boat—and our log booms—remained safe and secure, perfectly sheltered in their bolthole. Only the great gusts of wind that soughed through the tops of the trees, that sent sheets of ripples across the surface of the bay, that caused the tug to glide away from the dock, straining at her mooring lines, were a reminder of the fury being vented on the sea half a mile away.

By the late 1930s the *Mary W* had been replaced by the *Hili-Kum*, a handsome new tug built in the style of a seine boat. My father had by now discovered that this type of vessel, with its big hold and its sizeable stern deck, was more practical for his purposes than a conventionally designed tug. The *Hili-Kum* was designed and built by my grandmother's shipbuilder brother James, and her materials were the best the sawmill could supply. Her entirely self-taught designer turned out a boat that towed well, and could carry nine thousand feet of lumber on her stern deck and still remain stable in almost any sea. She was fifty-seven feet long and had a 75-hp Atlas Imperial diesel engine; her name meant "trustworthy" in the Kwakiutl language and she was.

The *Hili-Kum* was a workboat. She was there for emergencies, of course, and she took us on picnics and outings, and occasionally on trips to Vancouver, but she was first and foremost a work boat, and as such she earned a good part of our living.

Her accommodations were spartan. Up in her bows, in the foc'sle, were four narrow bunks with only enough headroom to get in and out of them. On each side, a porthole with glass so thick and scratched that it was opaque, admitted a little feeble light. Aft of the foc'sle was the engine-room containing the big Atlas, a bank of storage batteries, an air compressor and a long workbench with an array of tools above it and under it.

The Atlas was an engine with presence; it stood five feet tall and threw an eleven-hundred-pound fly-wheel. The camshaft opened the valves with a reassuring "ta-pocketa, ta-pocketa" sound that was a lot easier on the nerves than the frenzied whine of the high speed engines that were to come.

Off the engine-room was the one convenience: a head with its complicated system of valves and hand pump, an apparatus that mystified and embarrassed most of our passengers. Aft of the engine-room and separated from it by a bulkhead, was a big hold with the shaft rumbling under its floorboards.

Above deck, the pilot-house had one high berth and a stool for the helmsman. There was the usual paraphernalia: big brass wheels for the engine-room controls, gauges, a searchlight mounted on the roof, the compass and the radio-telephone.

Much later, on my father's new boat, the *Gikumi*, radar was added to the pilot-house equipment. Until the novelty wore off, we gazed with fascination at the sweeping red line and at the tiny dots that appeared here and there on its screen. One day, soon after it was installed, my father was peering into its depths, trying to get a feel for its navigational usefulness, and got so caught up in the wonder of it all that when he finally raised his eyes he found the *Gikumi* almost on top of a hapless troller. He had forgotten that a wooden boat wouldn't show up on the radar screen. He spun the wheel, the *Gikumi* veered sharply to starboard and surged past the smaller boat where the fisherman, white with fright and anger, yelled obscenities.

Aft of the pilot-house there was a cabin with a double bunk. The charts were in a drawer beneath it, and the chart table dropped from the wall above it. Aft of that, in the galley, there was a square Seacook stove with a rail around its top and a small stainless

The *Hili-Kum* under construction on Jim Sharpe's ways at Alert Bay

steel sink with a hand pump that delivered cold water. There were lockers for dishes and food, a long table and a bench. One of my friends, inspecting the boat years later, said that the accommodations reminded her of a refugee camp. Yet, even as a small child, I loved "the boat" with a passion. Pete Fletcher, writing for *The Westcoast Mariner*, said, "The highest moments of seat-of-the-pants adventure, pure fright and outright humour, occur on the sea in small boats." From an early age I knew that to be true.

"Time and tide wait for no man," my father would groan, getting out of a warm bed at four in the morning to catch a tide. Then he—and I as often as I could—would let ourselves out of the house and descend the long flight of stairs to the dock, where Jimmy was waiting in the damp morning air. We would climb down the ladder to the boat, the rungs clammy with moisture. The mooring lines dripped cold sea-water; even the boat's cabin was dank and cold. But within minutes, the big engine was thundering away, filling the air with the hot, rich smell of diesel and, just a few more minutes later, the galley stove was muttering and the coffee perking. The galley, so recently cold, soon became so uncomfortably hot that the door had to be fastened open. Outside, the boat thrust forward purposefully; the deck vibrated with the power of her engine; the wake hissed by; the air blew fresh and briny.

In the pilot-house, my father, who had complained so extravagantly such a short time before, steered with one hand and drank coffee with the other, happier than any man had a right to be. And so for endless days, lapis lazuli summer ones and leaden winter

ones, we sat on those high seats in the pilot-house and saw the natural world unfold. We watched the sun split the horizon, bringing with it a brisk little breeze that rippled the water and sent glittering light all over its surface. At the other end of the day, we watched the sun drop back into the sea, staining the sky with improbable colour and then, confidently, we sailed straight on through the inky darkness.

We watched pods of killer whales rolling along on mysterious errands, their glistening black backs curving smoothly out of the sea, and sometimes we were

The *Hili-Kum* entering Telegraph Cove.

Al Gauthier, Colin Armitage and my father's partner, Alex MacDonald in the millyard.

accompanied by porpoises, shooting back and forth under our bows. Seabirds bobbed along on the waves beside us or sat in solemn rows on bits of driftwood. We threaded our way past tiny tufts of green islands and sometimes, close in to shore to take advantage of a back eddy, we could almost reach out and touch the Spanish moss that trailed from the big cedars.

My father took guests along on these voyages whenever possible, often a group of off-duty nurses from the local hospital. Sometimes they had idyllic trips; sometimes quite the opposite, for my father couldn't control the weather and most of the guests failed to recognize the important part it could play in such outings. As a consequence, the passengers sometimes climbed aboard as a merry band and returned as virtual stretcher cases. One horrendous day in Queen Charlotte Strait, inching our way down from Fort Rupert with an empty scow, I was sent to check on one of our passengers who was lying on a bunk in the stateroom. Actually, "lying" was a euphemism. As the boat slammed down into the trough of the sea, her whole body was raised as if by levitation and then dropped back onto the mattress with a *thud*. I bent over her, clinging to whatever would prevent me from falling on top of her. She opened her eyes. "How are the other girls?" she asked. They were all, I told her,

desperately sick.

"Hell's bells, the poor sinners," said the occupant of the bunk, and turned her face to the wall.

However it's an ill wind, if you'll pardon the expression, that blows nobody any good. Whenever I stepped aboard the boat, Jimmy abdicated his role as cook and passed that responsibility on to me. As engineer, he hated getting meals, especially for guests; as a teenager, I wasn't a lot more enthusiastic about the job, or a lot more experienced than he was. In consequence, I was always discreetly delighted when our passengers began showing signs of acute *mal de mer*. It meant that I could proceed with meal preparation for three rather than for two or three times that number. In the heaving galley, Jimmy would affix an extra bar to the top of the stove to hold the pots in place, and I would wet down a couple of dish towels, spread them on the table and lay out the cutlery, secure in the knowledge that my culinary efforts wouldn't be scrutinized by strangers.

One of the mill's big customers was the Indian Affairs Department. They bought thousands of feet of lumber and countless building supplies, and the beauty of it was that, since it was a government agency, we got paid without having to resort to searching the local beer parlours to collect our receivables. The only problem lay in the delivery. Since it took at least three to unload the boat and our tug carried a crew of two, we relied on the customers themselves to give us a hand at the receiving end. The problem was that, at the Indian villages, there was seldom anyone there to help; in fishing season, there was *never* anyone there to help. Before one trip to Kingcome Inlet, my father made searching inquiries of the Indian agent regarding the docking facilities and the help that would be available. Despite the agent's assurances, we arrived to find a very small float moored to the shore and not another living thing in sight except two starving dogs who greeted our arrival with pathetic enthusiasm.

There was nothing to be done but to somehow struggle that deckload—all nine thousand feet of it—onto the float. As the pile of lumber rose, the float sank, until it was completely submerged. Then, with some difficulty, the tug cast off her lines (now some feet under water) and very gently, so that her wake wouldn't cause the whole lot to tip over into the sea, moved out into the inlet. That much of that lumber ever survived to become part of a house is doubtful. Certainly the shrinkage in any such building, as the sodden lumber dried out, would have been phenomenal.

For a while we operated a shingle mill as well as a sawmill, but when the Hadleys started their little shingle mill down Baronet Passage I guess it was easier to buy shingles from them for resale. Besides, just having a conversation with Merle Hadley was worth the trip. Like Pesnic, Hadley had a distinctive delivery. He spoke in such a slow drawl, and had such laconic comments to make, that anything he had to say turned out to be vastly entertaining.

When the *Hili-Kum* arrived at their place to load shingles, we always found their two little boys playing around in a dinghy, their float house immaculate and Hadley and his wife working together in the shingle mill. Merle cut the shingles; his wife packed them into bundles. Their movements were swift and sure.

Mrs. Hadley was a pretty woman with a beautiful complexion and smooth, dark brown hair. Her well-worn overalls revealed a small curvy body. As Jimmy and Hadley and my father trekked across the float with bundles of shingles they chatted.

"You're darn lucky, Merle," said my father, "to have such a hard working wife."

"Yeeaas," said Hadley, "aand she's the most eee-ven tempered woman in the wooorld—maaa-d *all* the time."

The *Hili-Kum* landing a scow on the beach. She would retrieve the empty on the next tide.

Several times a year, the *Hili-Kum* made the twenty-two-hour trip to Vancouver. To make these trips pay for themselves, she carried freight both ways. Going south, she carried a load of door stock to be delivered to E.A Sauder; on the return journey, her hold and her deck were piled with plywood, mouldings, doors and windows, for we now sold building materials as well as lumber.

Like the tortoise, slowly but surely, the *Hili-Kum* chugged down Johnstone Strait, through Greene Point Rapids and the Yucultas, past Cortes Island and Savary Island, and into the Gulf of Georgia. She pushed on past Sechelt, Howe Sound and Point Atkinson, past the houses that now appeared dotting the hillsides of West Vancouver, and under the arc of Lions Gate Bridge. Now, unfamiliar city smells wafted from the shore—the smell of industry, of coffee roasting, of automobile exhaust. Turning to starboard, she passed the floating oil stations and found a berth at one of the crowded floats in Coal Harbour. Once she was safely moored, her passengers and crew prepared to face the culture shock that they knew awaited them. Five minutes from the *Hili-Kum's* deck the chaos that was Georgia Street roared by. Legs still sagging from the motion of the sea, we found the stream of traffic always took some getting used to. Cars shot at us from all directions, but navigating cautiously, we reached the safety of the Stanley Park streetcar and were borne toward the dazzle of downtown Vancouver. For us, the dazzle didn't include hotels or restaurants. "Waste not, want not," was my grandmother's motto and we all subscribed to it. Accommodation ashore would most certainly have been an extravagance, so those on the boat stayed on the boat and ate their meals there. This could be confining and dismal in winter, but in summer it was pleasant to leave the noise and confusion of the city behind and have a cool, quiet dinner on the stern deck. Across the harbour lay the lush greenery of Stanley Park; the screams of its peacocks and snatches of music from Malkin Bowl drifted across to us on the breeze. On the water, the sculls from the Vancouver Rowing Club skimmed by on practice runs.

When we were children in school, my sister and I didn't go on many of these trips to the city, but in the spring of 1939 our parents made a startling announcement. They told us that the King and Queen were to visit Vancouver in May and not only had they planned the next trip "to town" to coincide with this visit, but they intended to take us out of school so that we could

make the trip and take part in the momentous occasion.

"This is a very historic event," my mother said, "and I want you children to have a lasting memory of it."

As it turned out, the trip did supply us with a lasting memory, but it was a memory peculiar to *our* way of life, not the Royal Family's; and it was my grandmother, rather than the King or Queen, who was the central figure.

There was just enough accommodation on the *Hili-Kum* for the family, grandparents included, and for Jimmy. We set off in high spirits with all our best clothes hung carefully on their hangers. Thanks to the Atlas these clothes, when we put them on two days later, would reek of Diesel oil. This rather marred our attempts to put our best foot forward, but it wasn't enough to dampen our enthusiasm.

As the boat neared Vancouver and entered the expanse of unprotected water that is Georgia Strait, we found a high sea running. The *Hili-Kum* reared and plunged and my mother, who hated rough water, predictably got seasick. After a while, she realized that her misery was being made even more acute by the penetrating smell of brass polish. Jimmy, anxious that everything be shipshape for the King and Queen, was polishing the boat's brass to a gleaming perfection. Mother crawled to the pilot-house and made him stop.

The rough weather was unfortunate for another reason. Our marine radio told us that the royal couple would be arriving on a warship at 3:00 p.m., that the harbour would be closed just prior to their arrival, and it wouldn't be re-opened to marine traffic until they had safely docked. This presented us with an unexpected complication. The seas had slowed our progress so much that we knew we wouldn't get under Lions Gate Bridge in time; in fact, off our starboard bow, we could already see four warships on the horizon, surging towards us from the west.

We decided to tie up in Caulfeild Cove and take a bus into the city. As the *Hili-Kum* struggled on past the entrance to Howe Sound and around Point Atkinson, all aboard, except the helmsman and my mother, were busy getting dressed in their best. Even inside Caulfeild Cove, there was a big swell running but the mooring looked safe enough for the boat. There was not another boat, or another soul around; presumably, they were all off preparing to greet the King and Queen. My mother's queasy stomach had delayed her a bit, but my grandparents and my sister and I were ready. We gathered on the back deck, which was rising and falling with the heavy swell, and my father and Jimmy stood on the float, which was also rising and falling quite markedly, and got ready to hand us down.

My grandmother went first. She reached out her hands to them, stepped forward—and the boat surged away from the float. What happened next was like a perfectly choreographed ballet. My grandmother missed her footing and dropped straight into the sea in the three-foot space that now appeared between the float and the boat. Still holding the men's hands—hers now high above her head—she disappeared below the surface. In the perhaps four seconds at their disposal, they yanked her all the way out and onto the float. Having reached the limit imposed by the mooring lines, the *Hili-Kum* hesitated, then surged once again towards the float. She heaved against it with the full weight of her heavily planked, sixty-foot hull, and the bumpers squealed.

Despite our way of life, I had never seen anyone fall in before. I raced to my mother in the galley.

"Nana has fallen in," I reported tremulously. "Right over her hat."

Before my mother could reply, Nana herself appeared in the doorway streaming water, her Madame Rungé suit a sodden mess. For some reason

it wasn't the condition of her suit—or her hat—that disturbed her.

"Well, I've just ruined my best corset," she announced sourly.

It occurs to me now that a person who has just escaped being drowned and/or crushed to death might be justifiably excused for suffering a shock reaction. It didn't occur to my grandmother—but she *was* upset about her corsets and about the fact that we waited for an hour, sitting on a low stone wall by the roadside, and no bus came along to take us to the city. And so we returned to the boat and continued our journey into Vancouver, tying up at our usual place in Coal Harbour, where we cooked our dinner.

The radio told us that on the following day the royal couple were to be in New Westminster, so next day we took the bus and sat in the bleachers at Queen's Park in New Westminster and waved little Union Jacks. The Queen wore a powder blue dress with a hat to match, and the King was in his naval uniform. As they drove slowly past, smiling and waving graciously, I reflected that neither the King nor the Queen had any idea how much trouble we had gone to, to be there for them.

Off our starboard bow we could already see four warships surging towards us.

VI

"AND HOW WAS YOUR DAY?"

The Blow Hole, a passage between the northwestern extremity of East Cracroft Island and Minstrel Island, leads into Clio Channel. The passage is narrow and shallow, and in it, near its southwestern end, is a rock which dries 17 feet. Kelp grows right across the passage. This passage may be used only by small craft with local knowledge.

British Columbia Pilot

That perfunctory question, "And how was your day?" took on a richer meaning at Telegraph Cove. How were our days? They were, in a word, eventful. We were fifty men, women and children cut off from the rest of humanity by forest and ocean. That, in itself, made our days demanding and unconventional. Add the perils of the sea and a whole array of balky machinery, and the opportunities for humour and drama were boundless.

At twelve, I wrote in my childhood diary, "Left at 12:30 p.m. for Bryant's camp. Enroute rescued Mackay's A-frame. Quite exciting and funny."

So there it was. Life was always either exciting or funny; often it was both.

On one date in my diary, there's the straightforward statement, "Morris Goodrow drowned at Bones Bay today." Morris Goodrow's brother Ed owned a pile-driver. Like his brother, Morris was wiry and dark. Their coveralls and mechanics' caps stiff with grease, their faces streaked with soot and grease and creosote, they seemed even swarthier than they were. Periodically, when our dock needed repairs, my father towed Goodrow and his towering machine into our harbour. There, against the dock, he and his crew heaved creosote pilings into place with a steam donkey, and then pounded them relentlessly into the sea bottom. It was heavy, dangerous work and, when they were working on the cannery dock at Bones Bay, it killed Morris.

We veered from tragedy to domestic misadventure. On the 22nd of one month I noted, "The *Alaska Prince* was in loading all morning. Mary fell off her back porch but mother says she didn't break anything. Fortunately it was high tide. [Mary's porch rested on

pilings over the water]. Our cat had kittens."

Just two days later, the entry is: "Pouring rain. Just finished dinner when Englewood called. Rush trip to the hospital with a man who blew himself up."

Small wonder that, as children, we had difficulty relating to our contemporaries in the city, for whom a strawberry soda appeared to be the highlight of the day.

For all of us then, adults and children alike, each new day presented fresh new challenges. Take, for example, one of my grandfather's contributions to the good of the cause. Being a yacht, and a wooden one at that, the *Klinekwa* was a high-maintenance proposition. Gone were the days when someone was hired to scrape her hull and apply red lead, or to paint and varnish her superstructure. So when my grandfather announced at lunch one day that he intended to spend the afternoon varnishing the interior of the *Klinekwa*'s cabin, his help was welcomed with enthusiasm.

With money in such short supply, a job like this never involved the purchase of a new can of varnish, as long as there were left-over dribs and drabs around. In fact, my grandmother's thrift was perhaps most noticeably manifest when it came to interior decoration. Embarking on a painting project, Mame didn't buy paint, but instead mixed together all the odds and ends that could be found. As a consequence, her bookcases were a dismal mauve-grey; and her wallpapering projects tested my father's paper-hanging skills to the limit. If a room's dimensions required six double rolls, he was never permitted that extravagance, but was supplied with five. He solved this problem with his usual ingenuity. Behind every door in every room the wallpaper was of another pattern. As long as the doors remained open, it was an effective solution.

So, after lunch, my grandfather, mindful of these economic constraints, dutifully searched the boat's lockers for leftover varnish. He unearthed a collection of containers, old pickle jars and jam tins, containing a variety of paint products. Finally, he found a tin with perhaps enough varnish in it to do his job. Lighting his pipe, he set to work. All afternoon he puffed and varnished, while the sawmill hummed companionably in the background.

When my grandmother had had her nap and her usual orange, she went down to the boat to inspect the project. The first thing she noticed was an inordinate number of flies stuck to the surface of the walls. Wet varnish is notorious for collecting dust and debris on its surface, but in this instance the problem seemed excessive. She went over to inspect my grandfather's operation more closely.

"Duke," she said in a fury, "you're a jackass."

My grandfather, ever one to humour the more volatile temperament of the ladies, stopped in mid-brushstroke and looked puzzled but benign.

"How *could* you paint this whole cabin with Roger's Golden Syrup?" said my grandmother, almost in tears. "If you didn't smoke that filthy pipe all the time, you would have realized this didn't smell like varnish."

It took a great deal of scrubbing to get it off and my sister and I refused to be conned into helping, even with the bribe of unlimited Orange Crush. As my sister said, "I'm not going to; I just *hate* all those bugs."

My grandfather was more successful in another of the roles thrust upon him by our isolated existence. He "did" kittens. This was necessary because my grandmother was a one-woman SPCA. She was continually rescuing starved, abused, or abandoned animals and then my grandfather was required to "put down" the unfortunates that were beyond redemption—and to do it in the most humane manner possible. This was easier than it sounds for, at that time, chloroform could be purchased over the counter. My grandfather must have been a bulk purchaser, since he spent a good part of his retirement years chloroforming cats, and became something of an authority on anaesthesia.

Of course, painting and doing kittens were Alfred Marmaduke Wastell's unofficial duties. Officially, he was a Stipendary Magistrate. When he was appointed to this position some government agency sent him a whole set of law books beautifully bound in tan leather. He kept them in a glass-fronted bookcase in the front hall, where they looked very impressive. I don't think he ever opened any of them, though. The crime in our area was pretty straightforward and he found that common sense and that ingrained sense of authority—or is it superiority—that came with being English was all he really needed.

My father's days were more varied, for he had many duties. He towed logs and delivered lumber, caught rats, cut our hair, supervised the bookkeeping, wallpapered our house and his parents', serviced the tug's big engine and provided impromptu ambulance and marine rescue services—all the while charming the endless procession of friends, acquaintances and strangers who appeared from nowhere and flooded through our house as inexorably as the tide. His only concession to his former profession was his firm commitment to a business shirt and tie, which he always wore, no matter how manual the labour. Even on the night the trim-saw building burned down, he was only prevented from completing his usual toilette by my mother who shouted, "For heaven's sake, Fred, forget your tie! The mill's on fire!"

There was an immediacy about our way of life—a very clear relationship between cause and effect—so that, when we were awakened at 2:00 a.m. by shouts and the crackling of fire, it was obvious to all that if the mill burned there would be no jobs in the days that followed. And jobs, in the 1930s, were highly valued. All and sundry, therefore, bent to the task of saving the mill. It was not easy. Our fire-fighting equipment consisted of a pump mounted on a large wheelbarrow-like contrivance and some lengths of half-rotten, second-hand canvas hose.

The first snag occurred when someone raced the pump from the dock at one side of the harbour to the mill at the other, only to find that the storage battery that powered it had been used for other purposes and was missing.

Someone else found a charged battery on the boat, hefted it up the ladder to the dock, and ran with it half a mile to the pump—not an inconsiderable feat when you reflect on the weight of a storage battery. The hose was lowered into the sea and the pump started. A more powerful pump would have burst the hose to shreds but, with the serendipity that ruled my father's affairs, the pump was just powerful enough to deliver water to the fire but not powerful enough to burst the hose.

Three things saved the sawmill: a) the tide was high so the hose, which was short as well as rotten, could reach the water supply; b) every inch of the surrounding area was in its customary state—sodden with rainwater (when it rains virtually 360 days a year, even a sawmill's combustibility is minimized); and, c) the building that housed the trim saw was some little distance from the main mill buildings.

This bracing interlude over, everyone went home to bed for an hour or two. At ten minutes to eight, the mill whistle blew as usual. The crew assembled, the machinery started to hum and the conveyor belts to clack, then at eight o'clock the starting whistle blew and the saws began to whine.

The millwright turned his attention to repairing what was left of the trim saw.

Not all disasters ended so happily. One dark winter afternoon when my mother had only been part of this new life for a few months, my father phoned her from Alert Bay. He had gone there in the boat earlier in the day and now, in the late afternoon, it was blowing so hard that he thought it better to stay put for the night. When it was too rough for him, it was too rough. His call spared my mother from worrying about his safety, yet it meant a long evening alone with her baby.

As she sat listening to a wind that was now literally shaking the house, she happened to glance out the window at the blackness that was Johnstone Strait— and thought she saw a light. She extinguished the lights in the room, stood by the window and strained to see. Out in the distant darkness there was, indeed, a light that flashed intermittently. She thought it unlikely that a boat would be out there in such a storm, and she was sure there was no beacon or buoy in that general direction. Puzzled, she watched for some time, trying to discern some pattern or direction in the blinking of the light. Finally, it disappeared.

Next day, the mystery was solved. A small open boat was found upturned, a larger boat was discovered aground on one of the Pearse Islands, and then the bodies of a man and woman were recovered. Instead of staying with their larger vessel when its engine failed, they had launched their dinghy and attempted to reach our lights across the Strait. The woman had put on her fur coat and a life-jacket and when her body was found she still clutched the flashlight she had used to blink her desperate SOS.

The night before, our boat had not been in her usual berth at the dock below our house, and it's unlikely that my father could have reached the couple in time had he come from as far as Alert Bay, although

The morning after the trim saw building burned down.

he most certainly would have tried. Yet my mother was haunted by that stormy night for a very long time. Years later, something would trigger the memory of it and she would berate herself once again.

"How could I have been so stupid?" she would say miserably. "Those poor people were out there calling for help. I thought of an SOS and I know the signal, but it wasn't an SOS—just a few blinks. I didn't realize that they were dropping down into the trough of those seas and then their light was cut off from my vision, and their message was garbled."

And then there was the night the light engine ran away. That is not to say that the engine actually left home. Rather the pin in the governor broke and the engine, accustomed to running at 350 rpm, began whirling around at three times that speed. The most immediate result was that all our lights flared suddenly from a normal level of illumination to a blinding white glare. Sensing that all was not well in the light plant department, Jimmy (who looked after this engine as well as the engine on the boat), set off at a dead run for the warehouse where the light engine was housed. In the few minutes it took him to get there, the screaming engine, vibrating uncontrollably, had shaken off its extremities. The exhaust pipe had snapped off and the day fuel tank had been ripped from its moorings on the wall and lay on the engine itself, where it was blazing furiously. The huge flywheel, almost a ton of spinning iron, was approaching its maximum potential and was ready for orbit.

"Oh my god," said Jimmy, surveying the scene, "what's going to happen here?"

It was a rhetorical question. He stepped into the maelstrom and pulled the wedges by hand and very gradually—for it had built up tremendous momentum—the flywheel slowed and then stopped.

If the engine had exploded, as it was very close to doing, it would have sent large chunks of iron and large chunks of Jimmy in all directions, and it would certainly have set the warehouse on fire, and possibly the whole town, for our fire-fighting equipment had done nothing but depreciate since the trim-saw burnt down.

However, the engine didn't do any of these things, and this brush with catastrophe didn't alter my father's habit of thrift one bit. The engine, obtained second-hand from the Marshall Wells boat, the *Sundown,* had been a good engine and he felt that the results of this little mishap—a flattened crankshaft and burnt out bearings—could be rectified. He phoned Tommy Penway, possibly Coal Harbour's best heavy-duty mechanic, and Tommy arrived on the Union boat and spent three days filing the flat spot on the shaft with a hand file and checking it with calipers. Then he replaced the bearings, told my father he had done all he could, and went back to the city. When the engine was started, it ran for only a few hours before burning out the bearings again. Undeterred, my father and Jimmy pulled the piston and forever afterwards this three-cylinder engine ran on two cylinders. The lights were never the same, though.

The passage of time did nothing to alter the drama of our days. In the space of a little over a year, the three Hanuse brothers were drowned off the mouth of the Nimpkish River, the Sticklands' boat exploded and caught fire, Hilly Lansdowne received a medal from the Humane Society for strangling the cougar, and John Nicholson's gillnetter was found drifting near Malcolm Island. John Nicholson was seventy-two. When his boat was found, the light on his net was still burning, as was his mast light. The engine and the stove were shut off. Having left things in good order, John had lain down in his bunk and died.

VII

THE AMBULANCE SERVICE

Baronet Passage—This narrow channel is entered from Blackney Passage northward of Cracroft Point, from whence it leads eastward into Clio Channel and Beware Passage, both of which are connected to Knight Inlet.

On account of the dangers within it, the passage should be used only by those in possession of local knowledge.

British Columbia Pilot

On stormy winter nights, the man who drives home on rain-slicked streets, puts his car in the garage and settles down with the evening paper, secure in the knowledge that if a crisis occurs in his immediate vicinity it will be handled by the appropriate authorities, that man is different from the man who settles himself with a week-old paper knowing full well that there are no appropriate authorities and that, if a crisis occurs in his immediate vicinity, he will have to take himself, and probably his boat, out into the gale. And the wife and children of the first man are different from those of the second.

As children, we learned very early on that in crises large and small we must cut the chatter and do exactly as we were told. Thus, if the boat was hurling herself into a bad sea and the helmsman suddenly handed over the wheel with the admonition, "Keep her heading just the way she is," and disappeared to attend to pressing matters elsewhere, we did just that. With a wheel as big as yourself and a wildly gyrating horizon, it might not be easy to follow instructions, but it certainly fostered concentration. If, on the other hand, some illness or emergency required us to cook dinner, we fired up the kitchen stove and got some kind of a meal on the table without scalding ourselves or the cat.

The real requirement was that we do whatever was asked of us—and sometimes a lot was asked—without protest or panic. In my father's books, "getting excited" in an emergency was the ultimate sin and, like all children, we wanted to live up to our parents' expectations.

Of course, it was easy enough for my father. He *never* got excited. He came from a long line of people who never got excited. His uncle James was a good example. Early one morning, before our parents were up, he appeared at our front door. My sister and I ushered him into the warmth of the kitchen where we were cooking breakfast, got him a comfortable chair and offered him coffee.

"No thank you," said Uncle James mildly. "I won't have any coffee this morning. I just want to see your father and tell him that the boat seems to be sinking."

If my father was calm, my mother was a contradiction. She had the nervous temperament of a race horse, yet when faced with a woman hemorrhaging her life away after childbirth, she was cool and in complete control. She was a registered nurse, the only source of medical help that was near at hand and, as such, her life was full of crises.

Sawmills are dangerous places to work; add the additional dangers peculiar to the sea, and you have the rich mix of disasters that presented themselves at our door. There were deep gashes and crushed ribs, fingers severed by the saws, and concussions from the force of flying objects. When the mill whistle blew a series of staccato blasts and the machinery was suddenly silent, mother braced herself. Sometimes, happily, the interruption was only a broken conveyor belt; but often, looking across the harbour, she would see a worried little knot of men surrounding some unfortunate. Within minutes they would be in our kitchen, or—if it was a stretcher case—at the bottom of our long flight of front stairs.

One man arrived with a finger that was hanging by just a few thin shreds of flesh. My mother returned it to its normal position and splinted it in place, and the tug took him to the hospital where the doctor sewed it back onto his hand. The operation was a success. The finger, he commented later, was always a bit cold and numb; but a finger is a finger, and even an unfeeling finger is better than none at all.

On another day, Norm, a tall, fair member of the crew, cut *his* hand badly; it was bleeding heavily so someone supplied an empty carton to catch the flow. He arrived at our door, holding his carton, just as Jimmy, the tug's engineer, was about to leave. Mother, seeing Norm's face, sat him down and whisked off to get some brandy. She returned to find Norm sitting there with his carton—and Jimmy out cold on the floor.

There were lots of "after-hours" medical emergencies, too. The 'flu that became pneumonia, terrible burns from red hot stoves, or the employee with the DTs who literally tore the bunkhouse to pieces one evening. And then there were the expectant mothers. Pregnant women were my mother's *bête noire*, that is, pregnant women who were nearing their due dates. In my mother's perfect world, they would all have gone to stay at the hotel near the local hospital a little beforehand and, when their time came, they would have gone to that hospital where there was the staff and equipment to deal with possible obstetrical complications—and there they would have been safely delivered. But they didn't. Instead they stayed at home until the last possible moment, then relied upon my father's skill as a seaman and/or my mother's as a midwife, to see them through their ordeal. This wasn't simply perversity. These mothers-to-be didn't have the money for extras like hotel rooms, they often had other small children at home to care for, and sometimes they didn't even speak English, and consequently felt safer in familiar surroundings. The interesting part is that the hospital was only five miles away which, by city standards, would be considered right next door. Like a conjuring trick, though, the perception of distance is not what it seems and can't be measured in immutable units like miles. Distance stretches and shrinks. In the city those five miles would be covered in a few minutes, rain, storm or shine, on a paved road in an automobile or ambulance. In our case, those five miles were five miles of temperamental salt water and the mode of transport was a ponderously slow tugboat. In the best of weather, the trip to the hospital took an hour; in a howling gale it would take a least twice that. And so, mother kept an inordinately sharp eye on the midsections of the employees' wives

and did everything possible—short of inquiring directly into their sex lives—to determine who was pregnant and at what stage. This was a cat-and-mouse game. In the 1930s, pregnancy was not advertised as widely as it is today. Quite the contrary. It was kept discreetly under cover until its presence could no longer be kept hidden.

It's ironic, then, that one of these tests of seamanship and midwifery took place at a time when my mother felt secure in the knowledge that there were no imminent births. She and my father were sleeping peacefully when someone came pounding up our long flight of stairs and started hammering on the front door. My father struggled into his dressing-gown and went downstairs. There followed a short animated conversation. Certainly it was animated on our visitor's part. He was practically shouting at my father. Hearing both our parents stirring now, my sister and I emerged from our respective bedrooms and met in the upstairs hall. Through the bedroom door we could see mother throwing on her clothes.

"A lady is having a baby," she said sweetly, ever anxious to put the best face possible on the brutal facts of life, "so you children will have to look after yourselves. Be sure to have a good breakfast, and be sure to close the draft on the sawdust-burner when you leave for school ... and get my box, will you dears, it's in the linen closet."

Her "box" was a wooden one, enamelled white. It contained packages of dressings and rolls of gauze bandage and adhesive tape, a sling and some splints, a bottle of iodine and one of aspirin tablets, a pair of surgical scissors and a thermometer, some string and bottle of brandy. These items, and her knowledge, were the first aid, and the last aid, she had to offer.

Both parents let themselves out the front door and started down the front steps to the dock. My sister and I stationed ourselves at the upstairs window. During the night, fog had filled our little bay and now, at four in the morning, we could barely see the end of the dock. Wisps of it drifted past the window and formed and reformed around the house. We could hear our father's brisk footsteps breaking the woolly silence as he went to rout out our boats' engineer and then, within moments, we heard the heavy thump of the diesel engine reverberating around the bay. We heard the "plank" as the lines were let go and dropped from the dock to the deck. The engine was put in reverse, and we heard the churning of water under her stern as she turned in the narrow confines of the harbour. There was a small boat moored to the front float. The *Hili-Kum* edged carefully alongside and the two boats were tied together. We watched as they moved away from the float—looking for all the world like a mother hen with a chick under her wing—and then disappeared into the fog.

As we learned later, the expectant mother was from a neighbouring logging camp. Logging camps seldom had boats of any decent size because all their towing was done on contract by large towing firms in the city. They had, at best, camp tenders used for pushing logs around in the booming grounds. This husband and wife had made arrangements to use this type of small boat to take them to the hospital. Since this was the first baby, they thought that if they left promptly at first contraction they would have ample time to get to the hospital. But they reckoned without the fog. Unaccustomed to travelling blind and with no courses to refer to, the boat's operator was lost within minutes. Sightless, they plowed around for a couple of hours, all three becoming increasingly agitated, and finally more by good luck than good management, they found our dock looming at them out of the fog.

My father, of course, had courses laid out for just such emergencies. He was, in fact, a fine seaman, but one would never have guessed it from his nonchalant approach. On a bright summer day, the boat loaded with lumber and with a full complement of the ever present guests, he would decide to run a course for that particular trip. He would check the compass and his watch and, while trading funny stories and eating a nutbar, he would jot down some figures on a chart or in the

back of the log book. Now one of these sets of figures took him unerringly to his destination.

Meanwhile, my mother was employing skills of another sort. As soon as she climbed onto the little camp tender and met her patient, she realized that it was too late to transfer her to the relative comfort of the *Hili-Kum*. So she sent the men for blankets from our boat and constructed a makeshift bed in the foc'sle of the smaller boat. Then, as the *Hili-Kum* felt her way through the fog, she straddled the camp tender's engine and delivered the baby.

Fred and Emma Wastell on the dock at Englewood—July 1939.

In the late morning, sitting at our school desks, we children could hear the *Hili-Kum* returning. We could hear regularly spaced blasts from her air horn out in the foggy void—first faintly and then loudly as her bows suddenly materialized out of the mist and she moved carefully into the bay.

Sound travels at 1000 feet per second, which is of little interest to the general population but can have great significance for the mariner. Before radar, when fog erased all reference points, a boat had only its whistle—and it's echo—to guide it along our intricate coastline. Courses could take you to your destination, but in fog so thick that only the bow of the boat was visible, the fine tuning had to be done with the whistle. Head out of the pilot-house window, ears straining over the sound of the slow-turning engine, the skipper blew his whistle, listened for its echo and felt his way forward. In theory, then, a one-second interval between whistle blast and echo meant the boat was five hundred feet from shore; but the interval was never timed—simply sensed from experience.

The entrance to our sheltered harbour presented a very narrow gap in the contours of the coastline. Approaching it in thick fog, engine idling, whistle blasting, we would hear the echo returning once, twice, three times. Then, as the boat edged slowly ahead and to port, there would be a fourth blast of the whistle—and silence. We had pinpointed the entrance. Around the lunch table we discussed the morning's events.

"Are they going to call the new baby *Hili-Kum*?" asked Bea.

"I doubt it," said my father.

My mother looked tired. "I've left the blankets down in the office," she told my father. "Will you have someone bundle them up and send them to the dry cleaners?" "You know," she added, "we don't expect to be paid for jaunts like this but I do think they might have offered to pay for the cost of the dry cleaning."

My father was confident on the water but never overconfident. When the straits were smoking with flying spume, he stayed home. Unfortunately those were often just the times he got called out.

A few miles from our little community there were two large logging camps. They had first-aid men, of course, and their camp tenders were equal to the trip to the hospital in good weather. But in a howling southeaster, they weren't—which is where my father came in. Our old crank telephone would ring and my father would go off in search of the tug's engineer. We would watch soberly as the boat left her sheltered moorage and headed out into the gale—even more

Two freighters loading lumber, one of them from a scow.

anxiously when her immaculate white cabin disappeared into darkness as well as wind.

The weather was not the only problem connected with these trips. Our boat was, after all, built as a tug not an ambulance and, as such, her cabin doors were too narrow to admit a stretcher. Stretcher cases then, which usually meant the most seriously injured, were denied the relative comfort and warmth of the cabin, and instead had to make the trip to the hospital lashed to the hatch on the back deck. To have been badly injured, to have endured the difficult trip out of the woods to the boat and then to lie on a hatch in the middle of a howling gale must have been a unique experience. The stretcher was covered with a tarpaulin and was securely tied down, but each time the boat plunged into the seas water would pour down the adjoining deck and out of the scuppers, and the propeller, racing as it lifted out of the water, must have shaken the poor victim unmercifully.

The other thing that made these trips difficult was the time they took. There were no public roads into the woods, no helicopters, no available float planes. Just getting an injured man from the site of the accident to our waiting boat could take many hours. One evening, our telephone rang with the message that the neighbouring camp had an injured man en route. The caller estimated that the crummy carrying him down the tortuous logging road would arrive within the hour. My father agreed to be there waiting with the boat for the last lap of the journey to the hospital. It was approaching 7:00 p.m. My mother was good at reading my father's mind.

"Who's going with you?" she asked.

"Oh, I'll just take the boat myself," said my father. "It's a nice night, no problem with the weather, and I don't want to drag Jimmy out after a day's work. Besides, it's not a stretcher case; the fellow on the phone said he thinks it's just a broken arm or something."

"Don't go alone," said my mother firmly. "Find someone else to go along if you don't want to bother Jimmy, but don't go alone."

As it turned out, my father and Jimmy were joined at the last minute by Stan, one of the mill crew, who decided to go along for the ride. And so there were three on board when they arrived to pick up their passenger—which was just as well. They found a logger who had been injured hours before and was in great pain; he had been given the first aid man's supply of morphine, but its effects had long since worn off. All the way to the hospital, it took the combined efforts of Jimmy and Stan to keep the patient from ending his misery by jumping overboard. As Jimmy explained, although no explanation seemed necessary, the man was Italian and "Italians are very hyper people." It was a tiring trip.

And then, of course, there was old Gordon Eiger, an ancient prospector who blew himself up with a charge of dynamite. On our weekly trips to Alert Bay, Gordon was a regular passenger. Bent and feeble, he would struggle aboard the boat and, once in Alert Bay, he would shuffle up the road to the beer parlour, buy half a dozen cases of beer and transport them back to his claim in the bush. One day we got an emergency call and arrived to find that he was the injured man, not that he was recognizable because for starters, he had burned all the skin off his face and arms. When he was bundled into a stretcher and onto the back deck, we were sure this was Gordon's last trip to Alert Bay. Several weeks later, we were stunned to see him tottering down the dock at Englewood for his regular run to the beer parlour.

On the raw frontier of the north Island, it wasn't surprising that injury and accidental death were such common occurrences. Our little local paper, *The Pioneer Journal*, was published in Alert Bay; almost weekly, it reported a litany of calamities.

"Witnesses say that the cable was rusted and it broke."

"It was thought that the log was stable but it was not."

"The boat was found drifting but no bodies have been recovered."

"The child was scalded to death when a drum of boiling water overturned."

Our own little community had few real tragedies, but we weren't entirely spared. In the very early days of the mill, a Japanese crew member slipped while loading lumber, fell off the dock, hit his head on the fender log, and was instantly killed. Much later, two boys escaped the adults' notice and were playing on the log booms that floated in the bay. Like all strictly forbidden activities, this one had an irresistible attraction. Nothing is more fun than racing across a log boom, hopping off one rolling log and onto the next before you can be pitched off into the water. One of them lost the game, was trapped under the logs and drowned. This saddened us all, not least us children, for we were a small group and the loss of one of us left a gaping hole in our ranks. We were sobered, too, by the realization that the retribution for disobedience could be so swift and final.

Then there was Jerry, a merry little boy with round, rosy cheeks and brown eyes that twinkled with mischief. He didn't live in our community but arrived each morning on his dad's gasboat to attend school. I remember that he stymied our teacher one day by telling her, in reply to her question, that his favorite colour was white. One day his father failed to deliver him to school and our teacher told us the truth.

"Jerry has died," she said.

We were shocked—but not too shocked to ask for further information. What had happened, we wanted to know.

"He ate too many salmonberries," said our teacher.

On the way home for lunch, we regarded the salmonberry bushes and their ripe fruit with deep distrust.

When I discussed it with my mother over the lunch table, her explanation was a little more technical, as a nurse's explanation would be.

"He had a burst appendix," she said, "and he didn't get to the hospital in time."

VIII

THE CREW

Dent Rapids is a stretch of turbulent water between the Dent Islands and the southern shore of Cordero Channel. It is 2 cables wide in its narrowest part and depths are over 50 fathoms. The tidal streams attain a rate of 8 to 9 knots with dangerous overfalls and eddies.

Duration of slack water in all the rapids is very brief and does not usually exceed 5 minutes.

British Columbia Pilot

If the Eskimos, surrounded by the stuff, have dozens of words for snow, then we certainly should have had more than one for rain. We were rained on for ten months of the year (and in August the fog rolled in). There was the generic rain that rattled out of the sky for days on end, and dripped ceaselessly from the trees and the eaves. There was the slashing rain that came with the southeasters; it gusted off the sea, tortured the trees, and crashed against our windows in furious bursts. And there was the drenching rain that fell, not in drops, but in continuous streams that had no beginning and no end. Beaten flat, the sea lay prostrate under its onslaught. The air was thick with its moisture.

The crew, depending on their natures, complained, ignored, cursed or joked. If they worked in the shelter of the leaky corrugated iron that roofed the mill, they were fortunate. If they worked outside, they bowed to the inevitable and struggled into their hot, heavy rubber pants and jackets.

In those dark Depression days, steady jobs were prized possessions. The mill offered twelve of them—but that was all it offered. The term "fringe benefits" hadn't been invented. Of necessity the initiative required of employees was astounding. Jimmy Burton's introduction to Telegraph Cove was not atypical.

Jimmy was the only child of a tiny, feisty Irish woman who had earned a living for them both cooking in logging camps and for railroad gangs. At nineteen, he had already worked on fish packers for several seasons but it was sporadic employment, and he jumped at the chance of a steady job on our boat. Late one evening, he boarded the Union steamship

Cardena in Vancouver with his bedroll, a six-dollar second-class ticket to Telegraph Cove, and the bag of sandwiches his mother had provided. His ticket entitled him to a bunk in the hold with the freight, but he decided instead to spend the night sitting up in the saloon. At some point in the evening he was engaged in conversation by one of his fellow passengers, a logger who was more than a little pissed.

"Want a drink, kid?" offered his new friend unsteadily but generously.

Up to this point in his life, Jimmy hadn't tried alcohol, but he felt that perhaps now was a good time to start. He accepted, the two repaired to the logger's cabin—for he was travelling first class—and his host poured them each a stiff rum.

Jimmy's next conscious thoughts were prompted by the cheery sound of breakfast chimes being played in the corridor outside the cabin. He discovered that he had spent a restful night lying on the lower berth of the logger's cabin. The logger, meanwhile, had spent *his* night folded up on the rock-hard, four-foot settee. The breakfast chimes had wakened him, too, and he wasn't in a particularly good mood.

"Who the hell are you?" he asked, belligerently.

"Don't you remember?" said Jimmy. "You invited me in for a drink."

Jimmy was by now ravenously hungry and would have liked to have hit up his erstwhile friend for breakfast, but it didn't seem feasible, so, refreshed by his restful sleep, he returned to the saloon where he sat down and ate his sandwiches. Before long, he discovered that he wasn't the only new employee on board. Doug MacLean was bound for Telegraph Cove as well. He was a year younger than Jimmy and had

had a gentler upbringing. This was his first experience away from home. At their destination, they disembarked together and searched out their employer.

Embroiled in the numerous tasks that "boat day" involved, my father was too preoccupied to give the two much of his attention. He did tell them that the bunkhouse was full, that they would occupy another building next door to it and then he sent them off in that general direction.

They found the building without too much trouble. It had no windows, no doors, no stove, no running water. It was March. "Jeez, it was cold in there," Jimmy remembers. There were several iron bedsteads with straw mattresses in the otherwise empty rooms. They selected the better looking of these and put down their bedrolls. Doug appeared disconsolate.

Jimmy & Thelma Burton, 1943

Walking through the freight shed on the way to this spartan accommodation, Jimmy had noticed some large flattened bread cartons. They returned to my father and asked if they could have some of these.

"What do you want them for?" asked my father, ever suspicious of any form of conspicuous consumption.

"Thought we'd tack them over the windows," said Jimmy. "Cut the wind a bit. Got a hammer we could borrow?"

Even this improvement—even the good hot dinner they had later in the cookhouse—failed to raise Doug's spirits. That evening he sat on his bed and cried. "Oh god, I want to go home," he sobbed.

Jimmy's experience in the college of hard knocks had made him a pragmatist.

"Well, Doug, how much money have you got? It costs twelve dollars to get back on the Union boat and it isn't even coming back for another week. I got no money. Nothin'. So the two of us aren't going anywhere. Tell you what, Doug," he said, "Let's give her a try."

My father eventually found them a little stove. Doug stayed till war was declared. Jimmy stayed for forty-eight years.

The bunkhouse that was too full to admit the two newcomers was not a great improvement over the place they presently occupied. It was an ugly board-and-batten building with a shed roof. True, it had windows, doors, a cold water tap and a big wood stove made out of an old oil drum, but it was a building inspector's nightmare. The sanitary facilities consisted of a privy that hung over the edge of the dock. The icy draft that blew in from the ocean below not only discouraged lingering, but had the disconcerting habit of blowing the discarded toilet paper back through the hole in the seat and whirling it around the occupant's head.

Wind whistled through the uninsulated walls of the bunkhouse, too, which meant that the crew kept their makeshift stove going full blast most of the time. Periodically, one of the

blankets from the *Hili-Kum*. Then she and my sister and I set off around the harbour to the engineer's house carrying our offerings. The engineer's house was, for convenience's sake, built right beside the mill, but we didn't find them there; rather, we found them in the blacksmith's shop. The father, a big raw-boned Scot, was frying eggs and bacon in a large, flat saw-dust shovel over the fire in the forge. He had scouted around and found some empty glass jars in the basement of the house, and they were using these as cups for the tea that he had made. It was obvious that they were a family not easily beaten.

When their possessions finally did arrive, we noticed that everything including their clothing had been shipped in barrels. Possibly a man's solution to the problem of packing up a household. At any rate, they were now able to set up housekeeping in their own slap-dash but cheerful way. It was plain that the children could have used a mother but, like their father, they were tough and resourceful and they proceeded to look after the household duties, go to school and somehow bring themselves up.

Several of the houses for married employees were occupied by Japanese families. They planted vegetable gardens which flourished despite the almost continuous rain, furnished their homes with furniture they made themselves, and built themselves skiffs so that they could row out into the strait and bring back a steady supply of seafood. Their food, fresh from the garden and the sea, was far more nutritious and much less costly than ours, but it never occurred to us Occidentals to learn from their example.

As the Depression ground on, men quite literally drifted in from nowhere. One cold winter morning, walking through the lumber shed on the way to school, my sister and I found a man sleeping on a pile of lumber. He turned out to be named Blackie. He had come around the point in a gasboat so old and decrepit that it promptly sank to the bottom in front of the cookhouse. Seeking drier accommodation, Blackie had removed himself to the lumber shed. When my father found him there later that same morning, he told him that he had better move into the marginally better shelter that the bunkhouse afforded.

Blackie was as swarthy as his name implied; he looked the type to be carefully avoided on a dark night. When questioned, he told my father that he was a flagpole painter, but that he had got into a little trouble and was advised to leave Vancouver. What kind of trouble was never made clear. Despite his murky background, he stayed and worked, and thoughtfully supplied my mother with some home-made ratfish oil for her arthritis. Except for one incident, he caused no trouble at all.

One evening, Blackie sat alone in his room, consumed a bottle of rye, and discovered in the process that life was an intolerable burden. He appeared at the door of Arnie's room carrying his .30-.30 rifle.

"Arnie, I've come to say good-bye," he said. "I'm going to kill myself."

Presented with this stunning news, Arnie's hands began to shake so violently that he could hardly pull on his pants. His mind, however, was working quickly and efficiently.

"Blackie, you'll have to say good-bye to all the crew," he said. "Not just me. You can't shoot yourself without saying good-bye to everybody."

So Blackie, carrying his gun, proceeded from room to room, bidding farewell to each startled occupant. He was down to the last couple of crew members and things were looking pretty desperate, when someone had another bright idea.

"You'll have to say good-bye to Alex," said someone with an inventive mind. "You just can't shoot yourself without saying goodbye to the boss."

Blackie was propelled out the door and sent off in the direction of Alex MacDonald's little bachelor house. Alex was a gentle and kindly man with a propensity for reading late into the night. He was more than surprised to open his door to an employee who was threatening suicide. But Alex was not a man to shirk responsibility. He invited Blackie into the living-room and, using all his powers of persuasion, tried to talk him out of ending his life. But Blackie was adamant.

"It's no good, Alex," said Blackie. "My mind's made up. It's not worth it. Life's just not worth it."

Alex, having lost the first round, now tried another tack. The night, he argued, was not the time to commit suicide. Nights were somehow not conducive to successful suicide.

"Wait till the morning, Blackie," he said. "Shoot yourself in the morning. You can see so much better in the daylight."

This made some sense to Blackie. They both had a cigarette while he considered the situation.

"Take my word for it, Blackie," said Alex, "the morning is the time to shoot yourself."

Since Alex was the authority when it came to cutting lumber, perhaps Blackie felt he was also an authority on suicide. At any rate, he was finally persuaded to wait for the morning and Alex accompanied him back to the bunkhouse.

Their entrance was regarded warily by the crew, and it was not until Alex had actually got Blackie into his room and into bed that they sighed a collective sigh of relief and went to bed themselves.

At 2:00 a.m. the blast from a .30-.30 shook the insubstantial walls of the building and, as a body, the crew fell out of their beds and formed a little huddle in the hall.

"Oh Jeez, he's done it," somebody said.

No one had the guts to open Blackie's door and face whatever lay behind it. They stood and shivered and smoked and whispered until someone got brave and inched open the door. Blackie lay on his back, his rifle on the bed beside him; there was a gaping bullet hole in the ceiling above the bed. As the others craned their necks to see into the room, their movements woke Blackie from a sound sleep.

"For Christ's sake, Blackie," said Norm, furiously, "what the hell do you think you're doing?"

"I tried to kill myself," explained Blackie, "but I missed."

And then in September 1939, war was declared and our little community was flung from one set of problems into another. For ten years, we had struggled with the spiritual and material impoverishment of the Depression. Then, almost overnight, we struggled with overwork and shortages. The most serious shortage was labour. Gradually, our younger crew members disappeared into the services, and the older ones left for higher paying jobs in shipyards and factories. And then, in 1941, the Japanese bombed Pearl Harbour and within months all our Japanese employees were gone.

Whether or not these people, given the opportunity, would have murdered us "round eyes" in our sleep remains a debatable question, for they weren't given the chance. Within days, they were required to pack up their possessions and be on their way to the Interior. For months afterward, many of their hastily packed cartons still stood piled in the warehouse. A month or two after one family's departure, a letter arrived. It had been, the letter said in laborious English, a difficult time. As soon as the family had reached their strange new destination, Kenny had

gotten sick and had had to have his throat cut. Since Kenny was their seven-year-old son, we interpreted this to be a description of a tonsillectomy. They asked my father to dispose of some of their possessions and to forward others to them and, in appreciation, they wanted us to have for ourselves "the flowerish cushion."

This final exodus left the mill desperate for crew members; my father and Alex turned to a friend in the city for help. Living in Vancouver certainly gave this man access to whatever labour supply there was; nonetheless, his efforts couldn't really have been termed a success. For one thing, he was a realtor and, as such, his knowledge of a sawmill's requirements was sketchy, to say the least. As a consequence, the results of his search for labourers were bizarre. He sent us men who could barely walk, let alone heft timbers. In his Mother Theresa phase he sent us a young man called Bing, a former inmate of a mental institution. He assured us that Bing would be able to function if a suitable job were found for him. Alex felt, quite rightly, that a suitable job was not one where Bing was surrounded by whirling saws. So he was made bull cook, and was supposed to help out in our garden when not otherwise occupied.

Bing turned out to be strong and cheerful, but he had a serious body odour problem and a genius for avoiding work. He also had a fetish concerning people's age. Since he had soon exhaustively interviewed all the crew in this regard, he was always delighted to see a new face—a face which usually belonged to one of our guests. He would approach them with a cheery smile, look them over carefully and announce, "I would say you're about forty-two." Since the person in question might often be a woman of thirty, this estimation of her age was not met with enthusiasm. Indeed, some found it deeply depressing.

My mother tried valiantly to avoid Bing when guests were present or, at the very least, to keep the conversation off the subject of age, but her efforts were to no avail. "Please disregard him," she would say. "Bing has a little problem," and she would wave her hand vaguely in the direction of her head. Despite this explanation, many of the guests were crushed by their encounter with Bing, and it took some time to cheer them up afterwards.

It was perhaps just as well that about this time the Royal Canadian Air Force arrived.

THE MADNESS OF WAR

Pearse Islands, a group of ten islands of various sizes and heights lying close together, are thickly wooded, and are located westward and northwestward of Stephenson Islet.

No attempt should be made to pass between the Pearse Islands, or between them and Stephenson Islet, unless in possession of local knowledge.

British Columbia Pilot

You've heard the phrase "the madness of war," referring to the practice of one group of human beings setting out to kill another. During the war years, we were mercifully spared the killing. We certainly weren't spared the madness, however, for we were suddenly introduced to the Military Mind. Our small, highly individualistic society had always been openly contemptuous of bureaucracy, and had existed largely out of reach of its clutches. Now it bore down upon us with full force.

Not that it started out badly. The Air Force decided to build an airport on an heretofore uninhabited stretch of land some fifty miles north of us, and the sawmill was to supply the lumber. Considering that my father had spent the previous ten years beating every conceivable bush for lumber orders, no matter how small—the bush or the order—this was an unbelievable bonanza.

There was one tiny hitch, however. In the years previous to 1939, to secure a lumber order and be promptly paid for it was the challenge. Securing the crew to cut the lumber required no effort at all. Now the situation was reversed. The airport construction would take everything we could cut—our total production—but putting together a crew to cut it was the challenge. Our able-bodied crew had filed off to war and the mill was struggling along, manned by the halt and the blind.

Nonetheless, this was an opportunity too good to be missed, and all the hands fell to with a will. Week after week, the crew loaded scow after scow, and the *Hili-Kum* edged them out of the harbour at high tide and started the long, slow tow northward, up Johnstone Strait and into Queen Charlotte Strait. In

summer, this was a more or less routine trip; in winter, southeasterly gales turned these straits into an unending procession of angry grey combers hissing with windswept foam. Going north with the loaded scows was the easier tow, for it involved a following sea; but returning with the empties was another story. Tug and scow now headed into the full force of the gale. Even with the engine slowed to half speed, the tug bucked and reared, water smashing against the pilot-house windows and running down the decks. Behind the boat, the scow was invisible behind explosions of white water, the towline tightening and slackening, the strain threatening to part it or—even worse—to tear the winch to which it was moored out of the deck.

Inadvertently finding herself present on one such voyage, my mother alternated between the pilot-house and the stateroom just aft of it. Most of the time, she lay prostrate with sea-sickness but, whenever some particularly spectacular gyration threatened to drown us all, she came reeling into the pilot-house to shout over the pounding of the engine and the roar of the storm, "Cut the tow, Fred, cut the tow!" My father paid very little attention to this momentary distraction.

Nor was the towing, itself, the only problem. The landing arrangements at Fort Rupert consisted of a hastily built grid on the beach, which meant that in the few minutes of high tide the empty scow had to be pulled off the shore, and the loaded one pushed onto it. This had to be done with precision; if the scows had drifted just slightly out of position, they would have got hung up and holed by the huge boulders that littered the beach.

Week after week the crew loaded scow after scow and the *Hili-Kum* edged them out of the harbour.

Other scows that had carried machinery and equipment up from Vancouver were often moored in the vicinity, and the Air Force sometimes wanted these juggled around. Usually the *Hili-Kum* and her crew were happy to oblige, but as winter approached and the weather worsened, the picture changed. One late January day, with the weather deteriorating rapidly, an RCAF officer appeared and began to bawl instructions from the dock.

"Take Number 43 out to the buoy, stand by Number 94 and then bring Number 63 into the lee of the dock."

His grasp of nautical terms was impressive.

My father was always patient and polite. "Sorry," he said, "there's a real wind getting up and I've got to get out of here."

He thought this explanation was sufficient. He was wrong. Under difficult conditions and in appalling weather, the airport project had been kept supplied with construction materials. The officer in charge was actually very fortunate in this respect, but he failed to see it that way. The problem, of course, was a deep and fundamental difference in philosophy. My father, who wouldn't have recognized an order it if jumped up and hit him in the face, simply ignored the unreasonable. For the officer, baffled and enraged by this seeming insubordination, an order was a sacred thing and left no room for a difference of opinion.

Given the season of the year, it was only a matter of time before the situation repeated itself. This time, short of manpower as usual, my father had enlisted Benny Brotchie as crew. Benny was a tall, impressive-looking native Indian who had the innate seamanship and laid-back demeanour so characteristic of his people. As my father leaned out the pilot-house window and manoeuvred the scow into place, Benny handled the lines on deck. Suddenly my father looked up.

"Oh Lord," he groaned. "Here comes our friend."

The officer, oblivious of the wind that was starting to come at them in great gusts, began bellowing instructions.

"Move Number 64 alongside Number 74, and then take Number 25 out to the buoy and bring Number 43 in."

"Got any more bad news?" yelled Benny as the *Hili-Kum* went full astern and hightailed it for home.

There were times, of course, when the weather was so bad that the return trip was out of the question. Then the tug, scow tied alongside, anchored behind the Cattle Islands until the wind subsided enough for them to venture forth. A phone message, relayed by some stranger, would advise my mother that the *Hili-Kum* was in the shelter of the Cattle Islands and would return when she could.

While the contractor was clearing the future airport of trees, and the laborious towing trips were creating an accumulation of building material, the Air Force administration was not idle. They decided, for some inexplicable reason, to run a telegraph system up

70

our rugged and uninhabited stretch of coastline. Unlike the earlier telegraph line that had simply been strung on trees along the shoreline, this new one ran further inland. There they built a series of line shacks, and manned them with airmen whose duty it was to patrol the line and prevent sabotage. These men were provisioned by boat, and the supplies they were issued were bizarre. They were given great bags of flour and slabs of bread, eight loaves to a slab. Presumably they were supposed to augment this carbohydrate diet by living off the land. Instead, they did what the Indians before them had done; they bartered with the white man. They hacked their way through the bush and presented themselves and their bags of flour at our store, where they traded for bacon or whatever other food appealed to them. Our Chinese employees always kept chickens. The airmen concluded their trading sessions by exchanging the eight-loaf slabs of bread for eggs and the occasional chicken. Years later, when the Chinese employees left, we found they had insulated their bunkhouse with the bread. All the exterior walls were stacked tightly, floor to ceiling, with dried bread.

The war brought other changes. Fifty miles to the south, York Island was fortified with gun emplacements. A military vessel patrolled the waters on either side of the island, accosting passing fishboats and tugs with a loud hailer and requiring them to identify themselves. Our first encounter with this new phenomenon was our most memorable. Since my father and his tug were known the length and breadth of the coast, he felt the burden of responsibility lay with the military. If they didn't know who we were, they could come alongside with their faster vessel and find out. Quite obviously, there was a difference of opinion. The military must have thought that *we* should be the one to make the effort, for one minute we were happily plugging along, my father in his usual tipped-back position, steering with his feet, and the next minute we heard a resounding boom and a shot was fired across our bows and landed with a splash in the water just off our port side.

"Son of a *biscuit* box!" exclaimed my father, knocking over the stool and slamming the boat into neutral.

He had managed everything this difficult coast threw at him—gales and reefs and tide races and fog—and his boat had never been so much as scratched. To be shot at was a hazard he had never anticipated, but such are the fortunes of war.

Since my father was often out half the night tow-

ing, my parents were not early risers. It was my sister's and my responsibility to get our own breakfast and to get ourselves off to school. And we were required to prepare a good substantial breakfast—nothing of the Pop Tart persuasion. So early one pitch black winter morning, with a howling gale shaking the house, we were busy making porridge and toast on the kitchen range and listening to the news on our old battery radio, when someone pounded on our front door. Our front door was entirely of glass, and it sometimes seemed that half the world presented itself, in full-length living colour, on the other side of that glass. Friends, customers, strangers, the injured, guests and employees materialized there with their various demands, requests, greetings and emergencies. On that dark morning, we looked through the glass and saw two young men standing outside. They were wearing sou'westers and oilskins, and water was streaming off them onto the porch floor.

We brought them into the warmth of the kitchen, offered coffee and listened while they told us how they'd got there. An Air Force boat, possibly one of the many tugs and fishboats that had been requisitioned, *had run out of fuel* somewhere out in Johnstone Strait in this raging southeaster, and these two had been sent off in an open boat to get help for the drifting vessel.

My sister and I listened, appalled. Even as children we knew three things: one, that to start on a trip without measuring the fuel was something only an idiot would do; two, that sending anyone out in an open boat in those seas was something only an idiot would do; and, three, that surviving a trip across the strait under those conditions was something only an excellent seaman would do. We were right on all counts; our two visitors turned out to be young Maritimers, which is probably the only thing that saved them.

We went upstairs to break this interesting news to our parents.

"Well, wonders never cease," said my father, getting out of bed, "Give them some breakfast."

While all of us ate a nourishing meal, my father and the Maritimers tried to establish just where their boat was when its engine stopped and how far, given the wind and tide, it might gave drifted. Then they picked up our boat's engineer and we heard the big Atlas kick into life and the lines drop to the deck.

For a few minutes, sheltered in the lee of the point, the *Hili-Kum* headed out almost jauntily, water churning out beneath her stern, exhaust whipping away from her stack. But then, as she emerged into the strait, the full force of the southeaster hit her broadside. Her mast swayed in a huge arc and her hull rolled until the red lead on her bottom was clearly visible. Finally, my father turned her with the seas and they began their search.

They careered along in a following sea for half an hour, seeing nothing but breaking waves. Apparently they had miscalculated; the Air Force boat must be behind them rather than in front. When my father was concentrating, he tended to hum to himself; now he hummed softly and searched for his window of opportunity, that small area in the seething sea where the waves were slightly less violent. Then he spun the wheel. The *Hili-Kum* didn't manoeuvre quickly; for a long few minutes, broadside again, everyone hung on for dear life. The chart table leapt from its fastenings and slammed down on the berth below and, in the galley, crockery, canned goods and pots crashed from one side of their lockers to the other. Then, heading into the seas, my father stopped humming and just steered into the oncoming waves. The difficulty now was to get a good look around. As the bows dove into the trough of the seas, water flung itself against the windows and poured down the glass, obscuring everything. But each time the boat shook off the water and rose on the crest of the wave four pairs of eyes—or to be more accurate, three and a half pairs, for Jimmy had an artificial eye—scanned the horizon for a boat painted camouflage grey in seas of the same colour.

Finally, the object of their search was spotted rolling wildly off to port. Jimmy went to attach a heaving line to the towline while my father, humming softly, manoeuvred the *Hili-Kum* into position. This wasn't the easiest thing to do. Nor was it easy to get the heaving line to its destination. The line snaked across the seas, hit the wet and rolling deck of the other boat for a second and then slithered off into the waves. Hand over hand, Jimmy yanked it out of the water as fast as he could lest it foul the *Hili-Kum's* propeller. The Maritimers stood ready to grab for Jimmy, should he lose his footing on the heaving deck. In the pilot-house, my father did a little ballet trying to keep the bows into the seas with the wheel, kick the stern into position with the clutch and keep track of the action on the back deck, all at the same time. After a couple of tries, the boats had drifted too far apart. The *Hili-Kum* made a wide circle and came in again, as close as was possible. Jimmy threw the line

once more. There were several men along the side of the Air Force boat now, holding on to the ratlines and the piperails. On the third try, someone caught the heaving line and pulled it in. Someone else helped to wrestle in the heavy water-soaked towline and get it fastened to a cleat on the bow. Jimmy and the Maritimers paid out some line, got it through the hook that hung from the boom, and secured it to the *Hili-Kum's* winch. The tow began.

As the two boats struggled toward the shelter of the Cove, my father reflected on our chance of winning the war.

"If our side can't even remember to fill their fuel tanks," he said, "I think we're at a distinct disadvantage."

As time went on, the airport contractor really got under way, and our rag-tag crew wasn't equal to the task of keeping Fort Rupert supplied with lumber. To solve the problem, the Air Force took over the mill—and the boat.

The *Hili-Kum* disappeared for a short time and reappeared with her glossy white paintwork painted a dark wartime grey, her mast bristling with aerials and her cabin roof piled with life-rafts. All this life-saving equipment wasn't as excessive as it seemed, we soon found, for the boat, which had always operated with a crew of two, now had seven on board. Apparently, the Military Mind deemed whatever number a boat would sleep to be the appropriate number for her crew. To my father's and Jimmy's astonishment, the *Hili-Kum* now had, besides her captain, a slew of mates, deckhands, first and second engineers, a radio operator, and a cook to keep this mob fed.

The same largesse was applied to the mill. Where our regular able-bodied crew had numbered twelve, there were now sixty-five. It certainly gave the place an air of purpose. Every house, as well as the bunkhouse, was packed with sawmill crew or "support staff." Carpenters arrived to build another bunkhouse and a huge mess hall, since ours was not nearly large enough to feed this army.

The individuals most markedly affected by this turn of events were our three Chinese employees. Our Japanese workers had long since been deported to the BC Interior, and the rest of the regular crew were in the services; but the Chinese, who had been with us ever since the box factory closed, were still with us. Now, once again, with very little warning, they were out of a job. They were old and their grasp of English had never been good, so other employment was out of the question. Welfare didn't exist. Nor did the three expect any regularized assistance. Instead, they adapted to this change with flexibility and imagination. They continued to live in the China House, which cost them nothing, they had all the free firewood they needed for fuel, they had always kept chickens and had a garden—and now they became bootleggers! Cut off from the nearest liquor store by miles of water, surrounded by the military, they followed the classic recipe for success: find a need and fill it. Their new occupation wasn't immediately apparent, for the dealings were always handled with the utmost discretion, but finally my parents realized where all those footfalls in the night were heading, and why. In theory this activity was not a good idea, because it took place on private property, the owner of which was my grandfather, the local magistrate. In practice, however, it all worked out, because all concerned maintained their ignorance, if not their innocence.

My parents' adjustment to the new regime was perhaps more difficult. Neither of them had ever had the slightest contact with the military, and for them it a was a dizzying transformation. Overnight, common sense, independence and thrift were replaced by foolishness, bureaucracy and waste—and, as my mother said, a distinct lack of neighbourliness.

"I find it very hard to understand why they don't offer to take us along when they're making a trip to Alert Bay," she said. "We always have so many errands to do there, and after all, it *is* our boat."

"It's not our boat," said my father. "The Air Force is leasing it."

"Fred," said my mother irritably, "you know perfectly well we have always taken along anyone who wanted to go to the Bay. It's just common courtesy. Besides," she sniffed, "In wartime you'd think they would want us to save fuel rather than have us use the *Klinekwa* when it wasn't necessary."

"Just be glad we have the *Klinekwa*," said my father.

The only good thing that came out of this, from my mother's point of view, was the fact that when the Air Force took our boat out, all of her crew were required to wear their life-jackets. Though theirs were the more glamorous "Mae Wests," this requirement made it easier for my mother to enforce her rule that my sister must wear hers, lethal though it later turned out to be.

At first, uncertainty over the course of the war and tensions over various scares and alarms made these new inhabitants seem a prickly lot. We were required to black out our windows, and one night we answered the front door to find two *armed* airmen on the porch. They told us we were showing some cracks of light.

"How silly," said my mother, going around jerking at the curtains, "considering the mill burner is blazing away all day and all night." Of course, she was right. The burner, the only such beacon in miles of dark coastline, pin-pointed our location exactly, and provided a perfect reference point for the whole area.

Gradually, however, we began to shake down and form a new community. The airmen ceased to be fighting men and became just sawmill workers and seamen; for some of them, this had been their prewar occupations anyway, and they reverted to them easily. And the shake-down took place more rapidly than it might have, because they all got the 'flu. Suddenly, half of the crew were seriously ill. No provision seemed to have been made for such an occurrence; there was only a first aid man who was as sick as the rest. So my mother quite naturally assumed her previous role of medical practitioner to the community. Granted, she had never had so *many* patients before—as she said, it was like doing hospital rounds. But she rose to the occasion with her usual unassuming efficiency, making daily visits to each bed with her thermometer, ordering fluids from the messhouse, dispensing aspirin and checking for pneumonia and other complications. Several of the men got serious nose-bleeds that were almost impossible to stop, but stop them she did. After that, both sides relaxed, and we began to go on picnics together.

What made these picnics such an event were the crashboats. Somewhere along the line, the Military Mind had conjured up crashboats. Perhaps it was an effort to keep up with the American Joneses who had PT boats, for that's what these boats resembled. They were seventy feet long, had twin 1400-hp Packard engines which raced them along at a dazzling speed, and they must have cost an enormous amount of money to build. They were the *Takuli*, the *Huron*, and the *Montagnais*, and one or other of them was always stationed in our little weatherproof harbour.

As the name implies, they were designed to come to the aid of planes that had crashed. Since no planes ever crashed, it made a very pleasant life for the crew—and certainly a very exciting one for us, for by now neighbourliness had set in and we were often slipped aboard for rides. Only someone who has spent her life on a towboat can imagine the thrill as the Packards thundered into life, and the vessel backed out of the harbour and hurled herself up the Strait, a great rooster tail of wake arching out astern.

To celebrate Dominion Day holiday, the whole community—for there were Air Force wives now, and children—formed a flotilla of RCAF boats and ours, and headed for the lighthouse at Pulteney Point. There had been a good deal of consultation over the locale for this picnic, because some of the airmen wanted to play baseball. This wasn't an unreasonable ambition, but it posed a problem. Open flat land, even a small plot of open flat land, is a rarity on the north coast. Pulteney Point is one of the few places that has a stretch of hummocky grassland between the beach and the trees. So that was our choice. The boats anchored offshore, and dinghies ferried passengers and picnic supplies to the beach. The last contingent had barely landed before the first to arrive made a discovery: the crisp, salty grass was alive with snakes! Disturbed in their peaceful isolation, they writhed away in all directions, causing havoc among the picnickers. The ball players weren't inconvenienced and some of the smaller boys were delighted, but the rest of the group confined themselves to a narrow strip of beach close to the water and complained bitterly for the rest of the day, because they weren't able to roam around without being attacked by garter snakes.

On an evening in August, we took our picnic supper to Pearse Island. Afterwards, in the starry summer night, the boats, engines throttled back, picked their way through the narrow channels by searchlight. The chart shows a cluster of small islands; between them are convoluted passages, some navigable and some choked with rocks. My father led the flotilla because he knew the way. Like Cyclops, the bright eye of his searchlight probed first one rocky shore and then swung across his bows to check the other as we proceeded through the maze. The cushions of moss and the gnarled trees that clung to the bluffs that hemmed us in on either side showed brilliant green in the white glare of the searchlight; then we emerged from the islands, crossed the black strait, and found our small harbour. We gathered our hampers and blankets, called our good-nights and climbed the long, wet ladder to the dock and the long flight of stairs to the house, and went to bed.

What these junkets cost the taxpayer in fuel, one shudders to think—but as a morale-booster they were a wild success.

Other occasions took on a distinctive twist, too.

The *Huron*—one of the Air Force's crashboats.

Our July 1st picnic at Pulteney Point.

One Hallowe'en night, after the younger children in the community had done their rounds of trick or treat, we were startled to hear a loud explosion. Looking out, we saw every building illuminated, every tree in stark relief, in the flickering blaze of a flare. The crashboat crew were providing a spectacular finale to Hallowe'en with their Very pistol. Adults and children alike watched with delight as flare after flare shot up into the night sky and drifted slowly down into the bay. It was a measure of our isolation that no one from the world at large responded to these international distress signals— and just as well, too. A breathless rescuer, arriving on our doorstep to discover that we were celebrating Hallowe'en, would have been considerably put out.

By August 1945, we were waiting, along with the rest of the world, to hear that World War II had ended. Although we expected the news, we weren't sure how quickly it would reach us or who would hear it first, for people with battery radios limit their listening. As it turned out it was Grace, an airman's wife who worked in the mill office, who broke the news. At four o'clock in the afternoon of August 14th, she heard an alert on the telephone. She picked it up and listened in. It was the word we had been waiting for. Within minutes, the mill whistle began blasting out its message to the mountains and the sea, to a wilderness that neither knew nor cared about the end of a war. One of the airmen fired off his rifle; the radios, now all on, blared band music; and, when the *Hili-Kum* came in later in the after-

noon, all her signal flags were flying.

The next day was a holiday. The community cooked, and the airmen prepared the mess hall. That afternoon, an air force swain found me out on an errand when he called around. For some reason, perhaps simply exuberance, he left me a note to keep me abreast of the preparations that had taken place. I have that note. It reads:

This morning we started in and swept the floor in the dining room part. I had been down earlier and took the ping-pong table apart and moved that awful old cot out of there. George set out to cut evergreens and we tacked them up on all the windows and at both ends. We've strung the boat's flags from corner to corner and tied the balloons up in the middle. We started out with about seven balloons and now there are only four. They popped for no reason I could see. We have put streamers up between the windows. The streamers are American Beauty colour. It looks just plain red in that light, though. The guys fixed up shades of the same paper for the lights and they look just like pantaloons. They bulge in the middle and have a frill around the bottom. Of course Harold had to criticize them but we like them so they stayed that way. We got sheets off the boat to cover the tables and I twisted streamers to put around the edges. See you later.

It was a great party, an innocent celebration. We didn't know, then, that we were marking not only the end of a war but the end of our isolation.

Towing the pile driver, c. 1954.

TIME AND TIDE WAIT FOR NO MAN

Crane Islands, three in number, lie about $3\frac{1}{2}$ cables northward of the eastern extremity of Bell Island, with a rock, covered less than 6 feet, situated about one cable northward. These islands should not be approached within a distance of 3 cables.

British Columbia Pilot

Someone once said that prospect of being hanged concentrates the mind wonderfully. In a less desperate way, and for a much longer period of time, a depressed economy focuses the mind as well. In the ten years from 1929 to 1939, everyone's attention was fixed on earning a living. We had a lot of home-made fun; every year my parents and most of the mill crew had saved enough for some kind of a holiday; my sister and I got dolls and books for Christmas; there was always plenty of food for ourselves and our many guests. Yet the overriding concern, the unspoken concentration, was still on having a job, getting paid, "making it" financially from one year to the next.

The war wiped away the Depression mentality. When it was over, everything had changed. Suddenly everyone had a good job and there was money to squander on things like outboard motors and record players. And, just as suddenly, everyone was tired of isolation, and began to push for a road that would connect us with the rest of the world. Getting a road became a collective obsession. Our local paper, *The Pioneer Journal*, exhorted the powers-that-were to do something and the powers-that-were gave speeches and made promises.

In the 1990s, things change with dizzying speed. In a year, an old log dump is transformed into a golf course, and a chic woman with a briefcase and a lot of jewelry is selling condos around its perimeter. Go away for a month, and you return to find that a whole chunk of forest has disappeared and a shopping centre is rising in its place. Forty years ago, change took place more slowly—so slowly that its presence was almost undetectable. Bit by bit, mile by mile, year by year, we got the road, but in the meantime life went on.

The mill, worn out from overwork, was repaired, the big Air Force mess hall became our community hall, the crew shrank back to its normal size once again and, a little later, my father replaced the *Hili-Kum* with a new boat called the *Gikumi* ("Chief" in the Kwakiutl language). We were so busy picking up the threads of our lives and getting things back to normal that no one noticed that "normal," itself, had changed.

Before the war, the *Hili-Kum* had ranged far and wide in her search for logs and customers. Her log read: Cutter Creek, Minstrel Island, Fort Rupert, Port Harvey, Knight's Inlet, Bones Bay, Scott Cove, Simoom Sound, Call Creek, Parson's Bay, Bute Inlet, O'Brien Bay and Loughborough Inlet, to name a few. We called at Bryant's camp and Mackay's, Soderman's, Campbell's, Sawchuk's, Wilson's, Bendickson's, Swanburg's, Carson's and Lafarr's. Now many of these small independent camps were closing, and the ones left were being annexed to huge timber companies with unfamiliar names like Crown Zellerbach and Alaska Pine. And so we bought our logs from these companies, situated right next door in Beaver Cove. There were no more arduous tows from far in the hinterlands. And the companies that sold us logs also bought our lumber—quantities of it, for they were building camps and logging roads all over the interior of the north Island. We supplied thousands of feet of bridge timbers—the most profitable kind of cutting a mill can do. But, of course, there was a dark side to all this good fortune. Because the mill was dependent on these companies for its log supply, its existence became dependent on their need for our lumber.

At the same time that these changes were taking

place in the forest industry, a whole new resource sector was springing up, bringing with it a whole new source of income for the *Gikumi*. There were iron and copper mines now in the Nimpkish Valley, at Benson Lake and on Neuritsos Arm. Huge Japanese ore carriers came to load at Beaver Cove and Port McNeill. When they sailed, they needed a tug to push them out and away from their moorings. Once under way, a Canadian pilot guided them through the Inside Passage until they came to Crane Islands and the open ocean. Here the pilot had to be taken off and returned to Port Hardy to catch a plane for Vancouver. And so the *Gikumi* took on, as well as her sawmill duties, the role of a sort of combined harbour tug/pilot boat. The job lasted for twelve years, and sometimes proved to be a demanding test of seamanship.

The first problem involved power. The ore carriers were enormous. The biggest of them, the *Yawatasan Maru*, was six hundred feet long and carried twenty-seven thousand tons of ore. Getting that dead weight moving was like trying to shift the position of an island. The *Gikumi* manoeuvred into position, placed her well-bumpered nose against the wall of steel that towered over her, and gave it everything she had. Water churned from her stern, but for a few minutes that was the only discernible movement. So

my father replaced the *Gikumi*'s Atlas Imperial with a new 290-hp Nissan.

"That thing will *never* last," Jimmy told my father. "It's just going crazy down there in the basement. Just a'screamin'. We'll see it come up through the decks any minute." Actually, it proved to be a very satisfactory engine but, after the Atlas, it took some getting used to.

Once under way, the ore carrier throttled back to allow the *Gikumi* with her maximum nine knots to keep up, and headed north. The *Gikumi* was on call 365 days of the year, which meant that on any one of those days—or nights—in fair weather or foul, the two vessels might follow each other out to the bleak tip of Vancouver Island. And before the smaller of the two got radar, it was a toss-up as to which weather was the most trying, fog or wind.

In fog, they lost sight of each other immediately. So the *Gikumi* would run her courses to the appointed spot in the ocean; then, with engine idling, Jimmy standing at the bows, and my father leaning far out the pilot-house window, they strained to hear the measured blasts from the Japanese ship's whistle. Having reached a consensus, they put in the clutch, revved up the engine once again and headed off blindly in the direction of the sound, Jimmy still standing

The *Gikumi* leaving Telegraph Cove and heading down Johnstone Strait.

The *Gikumi* alongside one of the ore carriers, waiting to perform her harbour tug duties.

outside in the mist. All of this groping about would have been easier if the vessels could have communicated by radio-telephone, but each was on a different frequency. Any conversations they had had to be relayed through a third party at the government stations at Bull Harbour or Alert Bay.

This difficulty was overcome by radar. At first, my father was highly distrustful of this new device. Nearing the appointed rendezvous, my father would say, "Jimmy, I think you'd better get out there and listen."

Jimmy, in his usual position at the bows, would concentrate for a few minutes and then point, "Yep, there's something blowing over there."

Taking a look at the radar screen, my father would say with astonishment, "Yeah, I can *see* it."

In short order, like a microwave oven, it became so indispensable that they couldn't imagine how they had functioned without it.

"Oh my god," moaned Jimmy, in mock dismay, "if this thing ever goes on the fritz, how are we going to make it out?"

Travelling at six or seven knots, neither vessel ever stopped throughout the whole procedure of picking up the pilot. In howling winter storms, this exercise proved more than usually tricky. The *Gikumi* was

given the lee side, of course, but in those exposed waters it gave scant protection. My father put the wheel over hard and shoved the *Gikumi's* front quarter straight into the side of the ship. The rubber bumpers screamed. Far above them the pilot, clinging to his rope ladder, timed his arrival. The *Gikumi* rose and fell like an elevator. He waited until she was on her way down and then came down the ladder hell-bent-for-leather in order to reach her deck before she started to come back up. If his timing was faulty, the *Gikumi* chased him right back up the ladder.

The most difficult feat was yet to come. In the wind, it was a formidable task to extricate the *Gikumi* from her limpet-like position against the wall of steel. She couldn't just slip astern, or she would be sucked into the propellers. She couldn't go right straight ahead, because she would get caught in the anchors or simply run over. Instead, her bow had to be gotten out into a position that would allow her to break away.

Given these circumstances, it wasn't surprising that the Japanese crew, sorry for the tiny vessel struggling so far below, were moved to acts of kindness. They sent lunches down to the *Gikumi* at the end of a heaving line. The first time one of these small boxes was lowered down to them Jimmy placed it carefully

79

The *Hosei Maru* raising anchor.

on the deck until the *Gikumi* had freed herself from the Japanese ship, then he took it to the pilot-house. My father opened it and peered at the contents.

"Well, Jim," he said, "what do you think?"

"I think them are the damndest sandwiches I ever seen in my life," said Jimmy.

"What do you suppose this is?" said my father, removing a capped bottle from the box and holding it up to the light.

"Tea?" guessed Jimmy dubiously.

My father unscrewed the cap and sniffed cautiously. "Cold tea," he said. "Tell you what," he added, "when that ship is right out of sight just toss this to the seagulls. You've got the lunch that Emma made for us back there, haven't you?"

"Why sure," said Jimmy. "Want a cup of coffee with it?"

"That'd be nice, Jim."

It's the thought that counts, of course, and the thought was very much appreciated. Nonetheless, as soon as the ore carrier was well out of sight, Jimmy threw "them crazy Suzuki sandwiches" to the seagulls, then laid out the peanut butter ones my mother had provided. Over the years those gulls stuffed themselves on sushi. It was enough to make a yuppie weep.

In 1948, BC Airlines based a Seabee in Alert Bay, and two years later QCA began *its* air service to the area. The mail now travelled by air, and great lumbering Stranraers carried passengers to the city and back. For the first time, a journey which had taken twenty-odd hours now took two. These planes changed the nature of medical emergencies, too. QCA was frequently pressed into service as an ambulance, and the

Seabee, while too small to carry a stretcher, was able to bring the doctor to his patients, thus supplying medical attention much sooner than would otherwise have been possible.

From the hospital in Alert Bay, Dr. Pickup was flown to accidents in many remote locations, but one of his most demanding emergencies took place at Beaver Cove, just ten air-minutes from the hospital itself. In March 1954, a crummy, returning to camp at the end of the day with its load of loggers, lost its brakes on a steep hill. The driver did the only thing he could: he turned the vehicle into the bank. It bounced against the hillside, rolled and then rolled again, strewing its passengers in its wake.

As soon as the news of this accident reached Alert Bay, Dr. Pickup and the BC Airlines pilot, Ed Bray, took off in the Seabee. There was a strong southeaster blowing, and if the take-off had been a bit dodgy, the landing was downright hair-raising. The pilot made eight attempts before he finally set the plane down on the stormy waters of East Bay.

Dr. Pickup found man one already dead and sixteen injured, eleven of them stretcher cases. Our phone at Telegraph Cove was ringing by this time; it took our boat, the camp tender and Robert Mountain's seiner, the *Tartoo*, to get them all to Alert Bay. At the hospital dock, a caravan of pick-up trucks and vans waited to transport the stretcher cases to the hospital where a little knot of men and women, recruited by the RCMP, were ready to donate blood. Those agencies and services which so effectively shield the city dweller from the harsh facts of life formed no part of our existence.

By now the little northern Vancouver Island communities, like eager ducklings, were making every effort to crack the shell of their isolation. Oddly enough, there was no shortage of roads. By the 1950s there were miles of good gravel roads snaking through the north Island. They were private logging roads built by the huge timber companies that had appeared after the war. The problem was that they didn't connect any of the communities, but simply reached into the wilderness to the timber resources. Their presence became the thin edge of the wedge, however, as we discovered at Telegraph Cove. In 1956 my father prevailed upon "Zip" Leino, the superintendent of the camp at Beaver Cove, and one day he sent a bulldozer operator over to punch his way through the woods to Telegraph Cove. There was no engineering involved, so the road wasn't all that well laid out; at our end water often poured down its slope into the mill yard. Nonetheless it was a road—a real road—and we were ecstatic. Now, on weekends, we could all escape the confines of that small cove. It was possible to *drive* through the wilderness that had been hidden from us for so long. We fished in the lakes, marvelled at the rushing glassy-green rivers, visited the mine sites, and met and made friends with people in the neighbouring camps. Now it was possible to go for a walk—not

Despite the language barrier, the Japanese crew member at the bow relayed his captain's signals and the *Gikumi* pushed.

a struggle through a trail hacked out of the underbrush, but a *walk* along a gravel road. Children could ride bicycles. Twenty years after the Superintendent of Education had envisioned it, children now went over that road to school. *Trucks* arrived from the two big camps at Beaver Cove to pick up lumber orders. On dark winter mornings a *bus* jounced down the hill and waited in the millyard, lights blinking, for school children to board it.

It was hard for us to believe. My father promptly bought a huge second-hand Chrysler. It had power everything, very little road clearance and was an entirely unsuitable car. He loved it. Several other of the Cove's inhabitants bought cars, including Jimmy.

Jimmy's choice of vehicle was entirely dictated by weight. He bought an Austin which was light enough for the *Gikumi*'s tackle to lift and drove it to Kelsey Bay, where it was loaded onto the back deck of the boat and unloaded onto our dock.

The Austin was a good car, but in time Jimmy was tempted by something bigger, and it turned out that his neighbour, Frank, was hot to buy the Austin. In fact, perhaps feeling that Jimmy might change his mind, or that someone else might beat him to it, Frank was seized by a sense of urgency. He arrived one evening while Jimmy and Thelma, his wife, were eating dinner and plunked a pile of cash on the table. He could barely wait for them to finish their coffee, so anxious was he to take delivery. He and Jimmy walked down to the lumber shed on the wharf where the Austin was parked, and Jimmy took all his fishing gear out of the trunk. The two of them got into the car, and Jimmy explained the esoteric English gear shift. Then, with Jimmy sitting beside him, Frank backed the car out of the shed, turned it around, hit the gas instead of the brake and flew over the twelve-by-twelve that edged our dock. It was a fairly low tide. The Austin did a flip, dropped ten feet and landed on its roof on the stern deck of the *Gikumi* moored below. Back in their kitchen, Thelma heard a resounding crash, saw the *Gikumi*'s mast arc wildly, and raced for the wharf. She arrived in time to see the two occupants crawl from the wreckage. Jimmy had hurt his ankle, but otherwise they were both intact. The car was not so fortunate; it lay smashed to pieces, its four little tires in the air.

Frank's enthusiasm for the Austin had waned; had, in fact, vanished.

"To hell with it," he said, or words to that effect. "Push it over the side."

Jimmy remonstrated.

"Push it over the side," repeated Frank, "I don't want it no more."

"Okay, Frank, I'll tell you what I'll do," said Jimmy. "I'll buy it back off you right where it is now."

Jimmy gave him seventy-five dollars of his money back. He sold the Austin's engine to an old fellow in East Bay for a light plant, and put the car's leather bucket seats in his boat.

The whole area continued to press for road access, and in 1962 a headline in the local paper read "North Island Dream Coming True." It went on to quote Dan Campbell, our MLA, who said that the government had approved a two million dollar highway construction project between Campbell River and Kelsey Bay. Further, the government had submitted

plans for a bridge over the Nimpkish River. By using the existing logging roads, this bridge would connect Telegraph Cove and Beaver Cove to Port Hardy. True, there was still a twenty-five mile gap between Beaver Cove and Kelsey Bay but now, at least, and for the first time, Kokish Camp at Beaver Cove could play baseball with the camp at Woss Lake.

"The north Island," said Campbell, "has been asleep for fifty years. This is only the beginning."

He was right, but we weren't out of the woods yet. The road progressed in a manner typical of the north coast. For one thing, it kept right on raining. Whereas, in earlier days when the interior forest remained intact, this rain had had little effect, it now washed debris down denuded hillsides and flooded rivers and roadbeds. When the Nimpkish River Bridge was being built, Vancouver Piledriving had their dredge secured by spuds: long steel pilings driven into the bed of the river. Heavy rains brought masses of debris down the swollen river and tore the dredge from its moorings. It was carried downstream, and finally came to rest on Flagstaff Island. The *Gikumi* was called out, and in the downpour and the dark they got a line on the dredge before the tide started to fall, and pulled it off the shore. By the early morning hours, they had it moored safely behind the breakwater at Alert Bay.

My sister Bea and Jimmy on the *Gikumi*.

Then another rainstorm washed out the Benson Lake road and left a gully ten feet deep across its width. Unfortunately, it happened after dark and a pick-up, driving along in the rainstorm later that night, fell into it. The passenger in the pick-up was knocked unconscious, the driver walked miles for help, and it took thirty loads of gravel to make the road passable again.

Periodically, school children had to get out of their bus and walk across bridges weakened by the rain, to transportation waiting on the other side.

Meanwhile, the twenty-five mile stretch of wild country that separated Beaver Cove from Kelsey Bay still presented an insurmountable barrier to the south. Once again, logging roads became the basis for access. There was only a little over a mile separating the north Island from Campbell River via the road to Gold River. When this mile of forest was penetrated we were connected—by a tortuous one-hundred-and-fifty mile gravel road that first zigged across Vancouver Island almost to its west coast, and then zagged in the opposite direction to the east coast. It was known as the Ho Chi Minh trail.

All these momentous changes—the roads, the air transportation—provided not only freedom from our isolation but competition for our faithful life-line, the Union steamships. Finally, on January 1st 1958, a large ad appeared in the local paper. Mr. J.A. MacDonald of the Union Steamship Company announced the end of its coastal service. He apologized "for the inconvenience this will create for our friends in the isolated communities of the coast."

You will note the word "friends." This wasn't a flattering term chosen by some marketing expert. It was a sincere description of the way the Union Steamship Company viewed its customers—and the feeling was reciprocated. The coast had lost a lot of its flavour.

Twenty years later, the mill at Telegraph Cove succumbed to these same changes. In 1940, the mill's advertising had read:

Telegraph Cove Mills Ltd.
Telegraph Cove, BC.
Rough & finished lumber for all building purposes
Mouldings, doors, windows, firewood
A private enterprise, buying logs locally and
Employing local labour
Write for estimates

It was a point of pride that the mill provided jobs and supported the local economy. By the late 1970s, neither of these things was important. Good jobs were available everywhere, logs were the exclusive province of the large timber companies, and the mill's huge circular saws were too old-fashioned and wasteful for an environmentally conscious era.

It was a gut-wrenching experience to close the mill, disperse the decrepit office furniture, and dispose of the files and the fresh white letterheads that lay in piles, waiting for correspondence that would never be written. It was years before I realized that this hadn't been a business. True, bookkeepers wrote paycheques, and invoices were sent out, and the letterheads said Telegraph Cove Mills. But it was not a business and never had been. It was simply a way of financing my father's great love, which was plowing around the coast on a boat. It was a means of supporting a way of life that had now ended.

Fred Wastell had followed his bliss without hesitation—without considering the effect that our isolated life had on his wife and children. As a result, Emma Wastell's life was one of relentless domesticity. There were no labour-saving appliances, no meals "out," no pizzas ordered in. Three times a day, seven days a week, there were meals—big meals—for if my mother was often lonely she was never alone; the house was always filled with people.

Given these circumstances, my sister and I were no strangers to housework either. We scrubbed floors, baked pies and did endless tubs of washing. That this was a type of forced labour was illustrated by an exchange between my mother and my sister when Bea was still quite young.

"Would you like to earn twenty-five cents, Beasie?" inquired my mother.

"No," said my sister.

"Well you're going to."

However, we had countless hours of pleasure and adventure too. Mine centered around the boat. Each time I stepped onto the deck's thick planks and felt the boat move gently under my feet, I knew I had found my place in the universe.

My father and I never discussed our bond. As a parent and child, our communication was limited. But generations of captains, on both sides of the family, had given to him his effortless seamanship, and to me my appreciation of it.

Our isolated life couldn't prepare us for the sophistication of the wider world, so when we finally did make our way into that world we were not, at first, confident. But for all that we lacked, much more was gained, because our upbringing had bestowed great gifts.

For one thing, I grew up to be "handy." Capability was not only highly regarded in our family, it was assumed. It was assumed that anyone, with a little effort, could do anything. And it was also assumed that those who didn't were either lazy or lacking in character—or both. So when the camp cook fell ill, I coped, at sixteen, with a massive wood-burning stove, a half-witted bull cook and a messhouse full of hungry men. Nor were the demands only domestic. In Victoria, I was sent on errands to the Capital Iron and Metal to find various esoteric machinery parts (at a good price of course), and in the summer, when Jimmy and his family went on holiday, I took his place on the boat.

The second thing our life provided was a grounding in reality. We came smack up against birth and death, against bravery and bullshit. As a consequence, I've never been able to get too interested in the superficial aspects of life—and I cannot be conned.

Thirdly, and finally, I received the greatest gift of all—the gift of nature. If, from infancy, wild country and a wilder sea are a palpable presence, they become part of the soul. I am grateful that they are part of mine.

Her tugboating days over, the *Gikumi* now takes visitors whale-watching in Robson Bight.